WILLIAM BLAKE (28 November 1757 – 12 August 1827) was an English poet, painter, and printmaker. Largely unrecognised during his life, Blake is now considered a seminal figure in the history of the poetry and visual art of the Romantic Age. What he called his "prophetic works" were said by 20th-century critic Northrop Frye to form "what is in proportion to its merits the least read body of poetry in the English language". His visual artistry led 21st-century critic Jonathan Jones to proclaim him "far and away the greatest artist Britain has ever produced". In 2002, Blake was placed at number 38 in the BBC's poll of the 100 Greatest Britons. While he lived in London his entire life, except for three years spent in Felpham, he produced a diverse and symbolically rich collection of works, which embraced the imagination as "the body of God" or "human existence itself".

William Blake

100 SELECTED POEMS

DELHI OPEN BOOKS

Contents

A Cradle Song

Sweet dreams form a shade,
O'er my lovely infants head.
Sweet dreams of pleasant streams,
By happy silent moony beams
Sweet sleep with soft down.
Weave thy brows an infant crown.
Sweet sleep Angel mild,
Hover o'er my happy child.
Sweet smiles in the night,
Hover over my delight.
Sweet smiles Mothers smiles,
All the livelong night beguiles.
Sweet moans, dovelike sighs,
Chase not slumber from thy eyes,
Sweet moans, sweeter smiles,
All the dovelike moans beguiles.
Sleep sleep happy child,
All creation slept and smil'd.
Sleep sleep, happy sleep.
While o'er thee thy mother weep
Sweet babe in thy face,
Holy image I can trace.
Sweet babe once like thee.
Thy maker lay and wept for me
Wept for me for thee for all,
When he was an infant small.
Thou his image ever see.
Heavenly face that smiles on thee,
Smiles on thee on me on all,
Who became an infant small,
Infant smiles are His own smiles,
Heaven & earth to peace beguiles.

A Divine Image

Cruelty has a human heart,
And Jealousy a human face;
Terror the human form divine,
And Secresy the human dress.
The human dress is forged iron,
The human form a fiery forge,
The human face a furnace sealed,
The human heart its hungry gorge.

A Dream

Once a dream did weave a shade
O'er my angel-guarded bed,
That an emmet lost its way
Where on grass methought I lay.
Troubled, wildered, and forlorn,
Dark, benighted, travel-worn,
Over many a tangle spray,
All heart-broke, I heard her say:
'Oh my children! do they cry,
Do they hear their father sigh?
Now they look abroad to see,
Now return and weep for me.'
Pitying, I dropped a tear:
But I saw a glow-worm near,
Who replied, 'What wailing wight
Calls the watchman of the night?
'I am set to light the ground,
While the beetle goes his round:
Follow now the beetle's hum;
Little wanderer, hie thee home! '

A Little Boy Lost

Nought loves another as itself,
Nor venerates another so,
Nor is it possible to thought
A greater than itself to know.
'And, father, how can I love you
Or any of my brothers more?
I love you like the little bird
That picks up crumbs around the door.'
The Priest sat by and heard the child;
In trembling zeal he seized his hair,
He led him by his little coat,
And all admired the priestly care.
And standing on the altar high,
'Lo, what a fiend is here! said he:
'One who sets reason up for judge
Of our most holy mystery.'
The weeping child could not be heard,
The weeping parents wept in vain:
They stripped him to his little shirt,
And bound him in an iron chain,
And burned him in a holy place
Where many had been burned before;
The weeping parents wept in vain.
Are such thing done on Albion's shore?

A Little Girl Lost

Children of the future age,
Reading this indignant page,
Know that in a former time
Love, sweet love, was thought a crime.

In the age of gold,
Free from winter's cold,
Youth and maiden bright,
To the holy light,
Naked in the sunny beams delight.

Once a youthful pair,
Filled with softest care,
Met in garden bright
Where the holy light
Had just removed the curtains of the night.

Then, in rising day,
On the grass they play;
Parents were afar,
Strangers came not near,
And the maiden soon forgot her fear.

Tired with kisses sweet,
They agree to meet
When the silent sleep
Waves o'er heaven's deep,
And the weary tired wanderers weep.

To her father white
Came the maiden bright;
But his loving look,
Like the holy book
All her tender limbs with terror shook.

'Ona, pale and weak,
To thy father speak!
Oh the trembling fear!
Oh the dismal care
That shakes the blossoms of my hoary hair!'

A Poison Tree

I was angry with my friend:
I told my wrath, my wrath did end.
I was angry with my foe:
I told it not, my wrath did grow.
And I watered it in fears,
Night and morning with my tears;
And I sunned it with smiles,
And with soft deceitful wiles.
And it grew both day and night,
Till it bore an apple bright.
And my foe beheld it shine.
And he knew that it was mine,
And into my garden stole
When the night had veiled the pole;
In the morning glad I see
My foe outstretched beneath the tree.

A QUESTION ANSWERED

What is it men in women do require?
The lineaments of Gratified Desire.
What is it women do in men require?
The lineaments of Gratified Desire.

A Song

Sweet dreams, form a shade
O'er my lovely infant's head!
Sweet dreams of pleasant streams
By happy, silent, moony beams!

Sweet Sleep, with soft down
Weave thy brows an infant crown
Sweet Sleep, angel mild,
Hover o'er my happy child!

Sweet smiles, in the night
Hover over my delight!
Sweet smiles, mother's smile,
All the livelong night beguile.

Sweet moans, dovelike sighs,
Chase not slumber from thine eyes!
Sweet moan, sweeter smile,
All the dovelike moans beguile.

Sleep, sleep, happy child!
All creation slept and smiled.
Sleep, sleep, happy sleep,
While o'er thee doth mother weep.

Sweet babe, in thy face
Holy image I can trace;
Sweet babe, once like thee
Thy Maker lay, and wept for me:

Wept for me, for thee, for all,
When He was an infant small.
Thou His image ever see,
Heavenly face that smiles on thee!

Smiles on thee, on me, on all,
Who became an infant small;
Infant smiles are his own smiles;
Heaven and earth to peace beguiles.

A War Song To Englishmen

Prepare, prepare the iron helm of war,
Bring forth the lots, cast in the spacious orb;
Th' Angel of Fate turns them with mighty hands,
And casts them out upon the darken'd earth!
Prepare, prepare!
Prepare your hearts for Death's cold hand! prepare
Your souls for flight, your bodies for the earth;
Prepare your arms for glorious victory;
Prepare your eyes to meet a holy God!
Prepare, prepare!
Whose fatal scroll is that? Methinks 'tis mine!
Why sinks my heart, why faltereth my tongue?
Had I three lives, I'd die in such a cause,
And rise, with ghosts, over the well-fought field.
Prepare, prepare!
The arrows of Almighty God are drawn!
Angels of Death stand in the louring heavens!
Thousands of souls must seek the realms of light,
And walk together on the clouds of heaven!
Prepare, prepare!
Soldiers, prepare! Our cause is Heaven's cause;
Soldiers, prepare! Be worthy of our cause:
Prepare to meet our fathers in the sky:
Prepare, O troops, that are to fall to-day!
Prepare, prepare!
Alfred shall smile, and make his harp rejoice;
The Norman William, and the learnèd Clerk,
And Lion Heart, and black-brow'd Edward, with
His loyal queen, shall rise, and welcome us!
Prepare, prepare!

Ah Sunflower

Ah Sunflower, weary of time,
Who countest the steps of the sun;
Seeking after that sweet golden clime
Where the traveller's journey is done;
Where the Youth pined away with desire,
And the pale virgin shrouded in snow,
Arise from their graves, and aspire
Where my Sunflower wishes to go!

America, A Prophecy

The shadowy Daughter of Urthona stood before red Orc,
When fourteen suns had faintly journey'd o'er his dark abode:
His food she brought in iron baskets, his drink in cups of iron:
Crown'd with a helmet and dark hair the nameless female stood;
A quiver with its burning stores, a bow like that of night,
When pestilence is shot from heaven: no other arms she need!
Invulnerable though naked, save where clouds roll round her loins
Their awful folds in the dark air: silent she stood as night;
For never from her iron tongue could voice or sound arise,
But dumb till that dread day when Orc assay'd his fierce embrace.
'Dark Virgin,' said the hairy youth, 'thy father stern, abhorr'd,
Rivets my tenfold chains while still on high my spirit soars;
Sometimes an Eagle screaming in the sky, sometimes a Lion
Stalking upon the mountains, and sometimes a Whale, I lash
The raging fathomless abyss; anon a Serpent folding
Around the pillars of Urthona, and round thy dark limbs
On the Canadian wilds I fold; feeble my spirit folds,
For chain'd beneath I rend these caverns: when thou bringest food
I howl my joy, and my red eyes seek to behold thy face--
In vain! these clouds roll to and fro, and hide thee from my sight.'
Silent as despairing love, and strong as jealousy,
The hairy shoulders rend the links; free are the wrists of fire;
Round the terrific loins he seiz'd the panting, struggling womb;
It joy'd: she put aside her clouds and smiled her first-born smile,
As when a black cloud shews its lightnings to the silent deep.
Soon as she saw the terrible boy,
then burst the virgin cry:
'I know thee, I have found thee, and
I will not let thee go:

Thou art the image of God who dwells in darkness of Africa,
And thou art fall'n to give me life in regions of dark death.
On my American plains I feel the struggling afflictions
Endur'd by roots that writhe their arms into the nether deep.
I see a Serpent in Canada who courts me to his love,
In Mexico an Eagle, and a Lion in Peru;
I see a Whale in the south-sea, drinking my soul away.
O what limb-rending pains I feel! thy fire and my frost
Mingle in howling pains, in furrows by thy lightnings rent.

This is eternal death, and this the torment long foretold.'

An Imitation Of Spenser

Golden Apollo, that thro' heaven wide
Scatter'st the rays of light, and truth's beams,
In lucent words my darkling verses dight,
And wash my earthy mind in thy clear streams,
That wisdom may descend in fairy dreams,
All while the jocund hours in thy train
Scatter their fancies at thy poet's feet;
And when thou yields to night thy wide domain,
Let rays of truth enlight his sleeping brain.
For brutish Pan in vain might thee assay
With tinkling sounds to dash thy nervous verse,
Sound without sense; yet in his rude affray,
(For ignorance is Folly's leasing nurse
And love of Folly needs none other's curse)
Midas the praise hath gain'd of lengthen'd ears,
For which himself might deem him ne'er the worse
To sit in council with his modern peers,
And judge of tinkling rimes and elegances terse.
And thou, Mercurius, that with wingèd brow
Dost mount aloft into the yielding sky,
And thro' Heav'n's halls thy airy flight dost throw,
Entering with holy feet to where on high
Jove weighs the counsel of futurity;
Then, laden with eternal fate, dost go
Down, like a falling star, from autumn sky,
And o'er the surface of the silent deep dost fly:
If thou arrivest at the sandy shore
Where nought but envious hissing adders dwell,
Thy golden rod, thrown on t 1000 he dusty floor,
Can charm to harmony with potent spell.
Such is sweet Eloquence, that does dispel
Envy and Hate that thirst for human gore;
And cause in sweet society to dwell

Vile savage minds that lurk in lonely cell
O Mercury, assist my lab'ring sense
That round the circle of the world would fly,

As the wing'd eagle scorns the tow'ry fence
Of Alpine hills round his high aëry,
And searches thro' the corners of the sky,
Sports in the clouds to hear the thunder's sound,
And see the wingèd lightnings as they fly;
Then, bosom'd in an amber cloud, around
Plumes his wide wings, and seeks Sol's palace high.
And thou, O warrior maid invincible,
Arm'd with the terrors of Almighty Jove,
Pallas, Minerva, maiden terrible,
Lov'st thou to walk the peaceful solemn grove,
In solemn gloom of branches interwove?
Or bear'st thy AEgis o'er the burning field,
Where, like the sea, the waves of battle move?
Or have thy soft piteous eyes beheld
The weary wanderer thro' the desert rove?
Or does th' afflicted man thy heav'nly bosom move?

And Did Those Feet In Ancient Time

And did those feet in ancient time
Walk upon England's mountains green?
And was the holy Lamb of God
On England's pleasant pastures seen?
And did the Countenance Divine
Shine forth upon our clouded hills?
And was Jerusalem builded here
Among these dark satanic mills?
Bring me my bow of burning gold!
Bring me my arrows of desire!
Bring me my spear! O clouds, unfold!
Bring me my chariot of fire!
I will not cease from mental fight,
Nor shall my sword sleep in my hand,
Till we have built Jerusalem
In England's green and pleasant land.

Auguries Of Innocence

To see a World in a Grain of Sand
And a Heaven in a Wild Flower,
Hold Infinity in the palm of your hand
And Eternity in an hour.
A Robin Red breast in a Cage
Puts all Heaven in a Rage.
A dove house fill'd with doves & Pigeons
Shudders Hell thro' all its regions.
A dog starv'd at his Master's Gate
Predicts the ruin of the State.
A Horse misus'd upon the Road
Calls to Heaven for Human blood.
Each outcry of the hunted Hare
A fibre from the Brain does tear.
A Skylark wounded in the wing,
A Cherubim does cease to sing.
The Game Cock clipp'd and arm'd for fight
Does the Rising Sun affright.
Every Wolf's & Lion's howl
Raises from Hell a Human Soul.
The wild deer, wand'ring here & there,
Keeps the Human Soul from Care.
The Lamb misus'd breeds public strife
And yet forgives the Butcher's Knife.
The Bat that flits at close of Eve
Has left the Brain that won't believe.
The Owl that calls upon the Night
Speaks the Unbeliever's fright.
He who shall hurt the little Wren
Shall never be belov'd by Men.
He who the Ox to wrath has mov'd
Shall never be by Woman lov'd.
The wanton Boy that kills the Fly

Shall feel the Spider's enmity.
He who torments the Chafer's sprite
Weaves a Bower in endless Night.
The Catterpillar on the Leaf
Repeats to thee thy Mother's grief.

Kill not the Moth nor Butterfly,

For the Last Judgement draweth nigh.
He who shall train the Horse to War
Shall never pass the Polar Bar.
The Beggar's Dog & Widow's Cat,
Feed them & thou wilt grow fat.
The Gnat that sings his Summer's song
Poison gets from Slander's tongue.
The poison of the Snake & Newt
Is the sweat of Envy's Foot.
The poison of the Honey Bee
Is the Artist's Jealousy.
The Prince's Robes & Beggars' Rags
Are Toadstools on the Miser's Bags.
A truth that's told with bad intent
Beats all the Lies you can invent.
It is right it should be so;
Man was made for Joy & Woe;
And when this we rightly know
Thro' the World we safely go.
Joy & Woe are woven fine,
A Clothing for the Soul divine;
Under every grief & pine
Runs a joy with silken twine.
The Babe is more than swadling Bands;
Throughout all these Human Lands
Tools were made, & born were hands,
Every Farmer Understands.
Every Tear from Every Eye
Becomes a Babe in Eternity.
This is caught by Females bright
And return'd to its own delight.
The Bleat, the Bark, Bellow & Roar
Are Waves that Beat on Heaven's Shore.

The Babe that weeps the Rod beneath
Writes Revenge in realms of death.
The Beggar's Rags, fluttering in Air,
Does to Rags the Heavens tear.
The Soldier arm'd with Sword & Gun,
Palsied strikes the Summer's Sun.
The poor Man's Farthing is worth more
Than all the Gold on Afric's Shore.

One Mite wrung from the Labrer's hands
Shall buy & sell the Miser's lands:
Or, if protected from on high,
Does that whole Nation sell & buy.
He who mocks the Infant's Faith
Shall be mock'd in Age & Death.
He who shall teach the Child to Doubt
The rotting Grave shall ne'er get out.
He who respects the Infant's faith
Triumph's over Hell & Death.
The Child's Toys & the Old Man's Reasons
Are the Fruits of the Two seasons.
The Questioner, who sits so sly,
Shall never know how to Reply.
He who replies to words of Doubt
Doth put the Light of Knowledge out.
The Strongest Poison ever known
Came from Caesar's Laurel Crown.
Nought can deform the Human Race
Like the Armour's iron brace.
When Gold & Gems adorn the Plow
To peaceful Arts shall Envy Bow.
A Riddle or the Cricket's Cry
Is to Doubt a fit Reply.
The Emmet's Inch & Eagle's Mile
Make Lame Philosophy to smile.
He who Doubts from what he sees
Will ne'er believe, do what you Please.

If the Sun & Moon should doubt
They'd immediately Go out.
To be in a Passion you Good may do,
But no Good if a Passion is in you.
The Whore & Gambler, by the State
Licenc'd, build that Nation's Fate.
The Harlot's cry from Street to Street
Shall weave Old England's winding Sheet.
The Winner's Shout, the Loser's Curse,
Dance before dead England's Hearse.
Every Night & every Morn
Some to Misery are Born.
Every Morn & every Night
Some are Born to sweet Delight.

Some ar Born to sweet Delight,
Some are born to Endless Night.
We are led to Believe a Lie
When we see not Thro' the Eye
Which was Born in a Night to Perish in a Night
When the Soul Slept in Beams of Light.
God Appears & God is Light
To those poor Souls who dwell in the Night,
But does a Human Form Display
To those who Dwell in Realms of day.

Broken Love

MY Spectre around me night and day
Like a wild beast guards my way;
My Emanation far within
Weeps incessantly for my sin.
'A fathomless and boundless deep,
There we wander, there we weep;
On the hungry craving wind
My Spectre follows thee behind.
'He scents thy footsteps in the snow
Wheresoever thou dost go,
Thro' the wintry hail and rain.
When wilt thou return again?
'Dost thou not in pride and scorn
Fill with tempests all my morn,
And with jealousies and fears
Fill my pleasant nights with tears?
'Seven of my sweet loves thy knife
Has bereavèd of their life.
Their marble tombs I built with tears,
And with cold and shuddering fears.
'Seven more loves weep night and day
Round the tombs where my loves lay,
And seven more loves attend each night
Around my couch with torches bright.
'And seven more loves in my bed
Crown with wine my mournful head,
Pitying and forgiving all
Thy transgressions great and small.
'When wilt thou return and view
My loves, and them to life renew?
When wilt thou return and live?
When wilt thou pity as I forgive?'

'O'er my sins thou sit and moan:

Hast thou no sins of thy own?
O'er my sins thou sit and weep,
And lull thy own sins fast asleep.
'What transgressions I commit
Are for thy transgressions fit.
They thy harlots, thou their slave;
And my bed becomes their grave.
'Never, never, I return:
Still for victory I burn.
Living, thee alone I'll have;
And when dead I'll be thy grave.
'Thro' the Heaven and Earth and Hell
Thou shalt never, quell:
I will fly and thou pursue:
Night and morn the flight renew.'
'Poor, pale, pitiable form
That I follow in a storm;
Iron tears and groans of lead
Bind around my aching head.
'Till I turn from Female love
And root up the Infernal Grove,
I shall never worthy be
To step into Eternity.
'And, to end thy cruel mocks,
Annihilate thee on the rocks,
And another form create
To be subservient to my fate.
'Let us agree to give up love,
And root up the Infernal Grove;
Then shall we return and see
The worlds of happy Eternity.
'And throughout all Eternity

I forgive you, you forgive me.
As our dear Redeemer said:
"This the Wine, and this the Bread."'

But In The Wine-Presses The Human Grapes Sing Not

Nor Dance

But in the Wine-presses the human grapes sing not nor dance:
They howl and writhe in shoals of torment, in fierce flames

consuming,

In chains of iron and in dungeons circled with ceaseless fires,
In pits and dens and shades of death, in shapes of torment and woe:
The plates and screws and racks and saws and cords and fires and

cisterns

The cruel joys of Luvah's Daughters, lacerating with knives
And whips their victims, and the deadly sport of Luvah's Sons.
They dance around the dying and they drink the howl and groan,
They catch the shrieks in cups of gold, they hand them to one

another:

These are the sports of love, and these the sweet delights of amorous

play,

Tears of the grape, the death sweat of the cluster, the last sigh
Of the mild youth who listens to the luring songs of Luvah.----

Cradle Song

Sleep, sleep, beauty bright,
Dreaming in the joys of night;
Sleep, sleep; in thy sleep
Little sorrows sit and weep.
Sweet babe, in thy face
Soft desires I can trace,
Secret joys and secret smiles,
Little pretty infant wiles.
As thy softest limbs I feel
Smiles as of the morning steal
O'er thy cheek, and o'er thy breast
Where thy little heart doth rest.
O the cunning wiles that creep
In thy little heart asleep!
When thy little heart doth wake,
Then the dreadful night shall break.

Day

The Sun arises in the East,
Cloth'd in robes of blood and gold;
Swords and spears and wrath increast
All around his bosom roll'd
Crown'd with warlike fires and raging desires.

Divine Image

To Mercy, Pity, Peace, and Love,
All pray in their distress,
And to these virtues of delight
Return their thankfulness.
For Mercy, Pity, Peace, and Love,
Is God our Father dear;
And Mercy, Pity, Peace, and Love,
Is man, his child and care.
For Mercy has a human heart
Pity, a human face;
And Love, the human form divine;
And Peace, the human dress.
Then every man, of every clime,
That prays in his distress,
Prays to the human form divine:
Love, Mercy, Pity, Peace.
And all must love the human form,
In heathen, Turk, or Jew.
Where Mercy, Love, and Pity dwell,
There God is dwelling too.

Earth's Answer

Earth raised up her head
From the darkness dread and drear,
Her light fled,
Stony, dread,
And her locks covered with grey despair.

'Prisoned on watery shore,
Starry jealousy does keep my den
Cold and hoar;
Weeping o're,
I hear the father of the ancient men.

'Selfish father of men!
Cruel, jealous, selfish fear!
Can delight,
Chained in night,
The virgins of youth and morning bear?

'Does spring hide its joy,
When buds and blossoms grow?
Does the sower
Sow by night,
Or the plowman in darkness plough?

'Break this heavy chain,
That does freeze my bones around!
Selfish, vain,
Eternal bane,
That free love with bondage bound.'

England! Awake! Awake! Awake!

England! awake! awake! awake!
Jerusalem thy Sister calls!
Why wilt thou sleep the sleep of death
And close her from thy ancient walls?
Thy hills and valleys felt her feet
Gently upon their bosoms move:
Thy gates beheld sweet Zion's ways:
Then was a time of joy and love.
And now the time returns again:
Our souls exult, and London's towers
Receive the Lamb of God to dwell
In England's green and pleasant bowers.

Eternity

He who binds to himself a joy
Does the winged life destroy;
But he who kisses the joy as it flies
Lives in eternity's sun rise.

Fair Elanor

The bell struck one, and shook the silent tower;
The graves give up their dead: fair Elenor
Walk'd by the castle gate, and lookèd in.
A hollow groan ran thro' the dreary vaults.
She shriek'd aloud, and sunk upon the steps,
On the cold stone her pale cheeks. Sickly smells
Of death issue as from a sepulchre,
And all is silent but the sighing vaults.
Chill Death withdraws his hand, and she revives;
Amaz'd, she finds herself upon her feet,
And, like a ghost, thro' narrow passages
Walking, feeling the cold walls with her hands.
Fancy returns, and now she thinks of bones
And grinning skulls, and corruptible death
Wrapp'd in his shroud; and now fancies she hears
Deep sighs, and sees pale sickly ghosts gliding.
At length, no fancy but reality
Distracts her. A rushing sound, and the feet
Of one that fled, approaches--Ellen stood
Like a dumb statue, froze to stone with fear.
The wretch approaches, crying: `The deed is done;
Take this, and send it by whom thou wilt send;
It is my life--send it to Elenor:--
He's dead, and howling after me for blood!
`Take this,' he cried; and thrust into her arms
A wet napkin, wrapp'd about; then rush'd
Past, howling: she receiv'd into her arms
Pale death, and follow'd on the wings of fear.
They pass'd swift thro' the outer gate; the wretch,
Howling, leap'd o'er the wall into the moat,
Stifling in mud. Fair Ellen pass'd the bridge,
And heard a gloomy voice cry `Is it done?'

As the deer wounded, Ellen flew over

The pathless plain; as the arrows that fly
By night, destruction flies, and strikes in darkness.
She fled from fear, till at her house arriv'd.
Her maids await her; on her bed she falls,
That bed of joy, where erst her lord hath press'd:
`Ah, woman's fear!' she cried; `ah, cursèd duke!
Ah, my dear lord! ah, wretched Elenor!
`My lord was like a flower upon the brows
Of lusty May! Ah, life as frail as flower!
O ghastly death! withdraw thy cruel hand,
Seek'st thou that flow'r to deck thy horrid temples?
`My lord was like a star in highest heav'n
Drawn down to earth by spells and wickedness;
My lord was like the opening eyes of day
When western winds creep softly o'er the flowers;
`But he is darken'd; like the summer's noon
Clouded; fall'n like the stately tree, cut down;
The breath of heaven dwelt among his leaves.
O Elenor, weak woman, fill'd with woe!'
Thus having spoke, she raisèd up her head,
And saw the bloody napkin by her side,
Which in her arms she brought; and now, tenfold
More terrifièd, saw it unfold itself.
Her eyes were fix'd; the bloody cloth unfolds,
Disclosing to her sight the murder'd head
Of her dear lord, all ghastly pale, clotted
With gory blood; it groan'd, and thus it spake:
`O Elenor, I am thy husband's head,
Who, sleeping on the stones of yonder tower,
Was 'reft of life by the accursèd duke!
A hirèd villain turn'd my sleep to death!
`O Elenor, beware the cursèd duke;
O give not him thy hand, now I am dead;
He seeks thy love; who, coward, in the night,
Hirèd a villain to bereave my life.'
She sat with dead cold limbs, stiffen'd to stone;
She took the gory head up in her arms;

She kiss'd the pale lips; she had no tears to shed;
She hugg'd it to her breast, and groan'd her last.

From Milton: And Did Those Feet

And did those feet in ancient time
Walk upon England's mountains green?
And was the holy Lamb of God
On England's pleasant pastures seen?
And did the Countenance Divine
Shine forth upon our clouded hills?
And was Jerusalem builded here,
Among these dark Satanic Mills?
Bring me my Bow of burning gold:
Bring me my Arrows of desire:
Bring me my Spear:O clouds unfold!
Bring me my Chariot of fire!
I will not cease from Mental Fight,
Nor shall my Sword sleep in my hand,
Till we have built Jerusalem
In England's green & pleasant Land.

Gwin King Of Norway

Come, kings, and listen to my song:
When Gwin, the son of Nore,
Over the nations of the North
His cruel sceptre bore;
The nobles of the land did feed
Upon the hungry poor;
They tear the poor man's lamb, and drive
The needy from their door.
`The land is desolate; our wives
And children cry for bread;
Arise, and pull the tyrant down!
Let Gwin be humblèd!'
Gordred the giant rous'd himself
From sleeping in his cave;
He shook the hills, and in the clouds
The troubl'd banners wave.
Beneath them roll'd, like tempests black,
The num'rous sons of blood;
Like lions' whelps, roaring abroad,
Seeking their nightly food.
Down Bleron's hills they dreadful rush,
Their cry ascends the clouds;
The trampling horse and clanging arms
Like rushing mighty floods!
Their wives and children, weeping loud,
Follow in wild array,
Howling like ghosts, furious as wolves
In the bleak wintry day.
`Pull down the tyrant to the dust,
Let Gwin be humblèd,'
They cry, `and let ten thousand lives
Pay for the tyrant's head.'

From tow'r to tow'r the watchmen cry,

`O Gwin, the son of Nore,
Arouse thyself! the nations, black
Like clouds, come rolling o'er!'
Gwin rear'd his shield, his palace shakes,
His chiefs come rushing round;
Each, like an awful thunder cloud,
With voice of solemn sound:
Like rearèd stones around a grave
They stand around the King;
Then suddenly each seiz'd his spear,
And clashing steel does ring.
The husbandman does leave his plough
To wade thro' fields of gore;
The merchant binds his brows in steel,
And leaves the trading shore;
The shepherd leaves his mellow pipe,
And sounds the trumpet shrill;
The workman throws his hammer down
To heave the bloody bill.
Like the tall ghost of Barraton
Who sports in stormy sky,
Gwin leads his host, as black as night
When pestilence does fly,
With horses and with chariots--
And all his spearmen b 1000 old
March to the sound of mournful song,
Like clouds around him roll'd.
Gwin lifts his hand--the nations halt;
`Prepare for war!' he cries--
Gordred appears!--his frowning brow
Troubles our northern skies.
The armies stand, like balances
Held in th' Almighty's hand;--

`Gwin, thou hast fill'd thy measure up:
Thou'rt swept from out the land.'
And now the raging armies rush'd

Like warring mighty seas;
The heav'ns are shook with roaring war,
The dust ascends the skies!
Earth smokes with blood, and groans and shakes
To drink her children's gore,
A sea of blood; nor can the eye
See to the trembling shore!
And on the verge of this wild sea
Famine and death doth cry;
The cries of women and of babes
Over the field doth fly.
The King is seen raging afar,
With all his men of might;
Like blazing comets scattering death
Thro' the red fev'rous night.
Beneath his arm like sheep they die,
And groan upon the plain;
The battle faints, and bloody men
Fight upon hills of slain.
Now death is sick, and riven men
Labour and toil for life;
Steed rolls on steed, and shield on shield,
Sunk in this sea of strife!
The god of war is drunk with blood;
The earth doth faint and fail;
The stench of blood makes sick the heav'ns;
Ghosts glut the throat of hell!
O what have kings to answer for
Before that awful throne;
When thousand deaths for vengeance cry,
And ghosts accusing groan!

Like blazing comets in the sky
That shake the stars of light,
Which drop like fruit unto the earth
Thro' the fierce burning night;
Like these did Gwin and Gordred meet,

And the first blow decides;
Down from the brow unto the breast
Gordred his head divides!
Gwin fell: the sons of Norway fled,
All that remain'd alive;
The rest did fill the vale of death,
For them the eagles strive.
The river Dorman roll'd their blood
Into the northern sea;
Who mourn'd his sons, and overwhelm'd
The pleasant south country.

Hear The Voice

HEAR the voice of the Bard,
Who present, past, and future, sees;
Whose ears have heard
The Holy Word
That walk'd among the ancient trees;
Calling the lapsed soul,
And weeping in the evening dew;
That might control
The starry pole,
And fallen, fallen light renew!
'O Earth, O Earth, return!
Arise from out the dewy grass!
Night is worn,
And the morn
Rises from the slumbrous mass.
'Turn away no more;
Why wilt thou turn away?
The starry floor,
The watery shore,
Is given thee till the break of day.'

Hear The Voice Of The Bard

Hear the voice of the Bard !
Who present, past, and future sees;
Whose ears have heard
The Holy Word,
That walked among the ancient trees,
Calling the lapsed soul,
And weeping in the evening dew;
That might control
The starry pole,
And fallen, fallen, light renew!
'O Earth, O Earth, return!
Arise from out the dewy grass;
Night is worn,
And the morn
Rises from the slumberous mass.
'Turn away no more;
Why wilt thou turn away?
The starry floor,
The watery shore,
Is given thee till the break of day.'

Holy Thursday (Experience)

Is this a holy thing to see.
In a rich and fruitful land.
Babes reduced to misery.
Fed with cold and usurous hand?
Is that trembling cry a song?
Can it be a song of joy?
And so many children poor?
It is a land of poverty!
And their sun does never shine.
And their fields are bleak & bare.
And their ways are fill'd with thorns
It is eternal winter there.
For where-e'er the sun does shine.
And where-e'er the rain does fall:
Babe can never hunger there,
Nor poverty the mind appall.

Holy Thursday (Innocence)

Twas on a Holy Thursday their innocent faces clean
The children walking two & two in red & blue & green
Grey headed beadles walked before with wands as white as snow
Till into the high dome of Pauls they like Thames waters flow
O what a multitude they seemed these flowers of London town
Seated in companies they sit with radiance all their own
The hum of multitudes was there but multitudes of lambs
Thousands of little boys & girls raising their innocent hands
Now like a mighty wind they raise to heaven the voice of song
Or like harmonious thunderings the seats of heaven among
Beneath them sit the aged men wise guardians of the poor
Then cherish pity, lest you drive an angel from your door

How sweet I roam'd from field to field,
And tasted all the summer's pride
'Til the prince of love beheld
Who in the sunny beams did glide!
He shew'd me lilies for my hair
And blushing roses for my brow;
He led me through his garden fair,
Where all his golden pleasures grow.
With sweet May dews my wings were wet,
And Phoebus fir'd my vocal rage
He caught me in his silken net,
And shut me in his golden cage.
He loves to sit and hear me sing,
Then, laughing, sports and plays with me;
Then stretches out my golden wing,
And mocks my loss of liberty.

I Heard An Angel

I heard an Angel singing
When the day was springing,
'Mercy, Pity, Peace
Is the world's release.'
Thus he sung all day
Over the new mown hay,
Till the sun went down
And haycocks looked brown.
I heard a Devil curse
Over the heath and the furze,
'Mercy could be no more,
If there was nobody poor,
And pity no more could be,
If all were as happy as we.'
At his curse the sun went down,
And the heavens gave a frown.
Down pour'd the heavy rain
Over the new reap'd grain ...
And Miseries' increase
Is Mercy, Pity, Peace.

I Rose Up At The Dawn Of Day

I rose up at the dawn of day--
`Get thee away! get thee away!
Pray'st thou for riches? Away! away!
This is the Throne of Mammon grey.'
Said I: This, sure, is very odd;
I took it to be the Throne of God.
For everything besides I have:
It is only for riches that I can crave.
I have mental joy, and mental health,
And mental friends, and mental wealth;
I've a wife I love, and that loves me;
I've all but riches bodily.
I am in God's presence night and day,
And He never turns His face away;
The accuser of sins by my side doth stand,
And he holds my money-bag in his hand.
For my worldly things God makes him pay,
And he'd pay for more if to him I would pray;
And so you may do the worst you can do;
Be assur'd, Mr. Devil, I won't pray to you.
Then if for riches I must not pray,
God knows, I little of prayers need say;
So, as a church is known by its steeple,
If I pray it must be for other people.
He says, if I do not worship him for a God,
I shall eat coarser food, and go worse shod;
So, as I don't value such things as these,
You must do, Mr. Devil, just as God please.

I Saw A Chapel

I saw a chapel all of gold
That none did dare to enter in,
And many weeping stood without,
Weeping, mourning, worshipping.
I saw a serpent rise between
The white pillars of the door,
And he forc'd and forc'd and forc'd,
Down the golden hinges tore.
And along the pavement sweet,
Set with pearls and rubies bright,
All his slimy length he drew
Till upon the altar white
Vomiting his poison out
On the bread and on the wine.
So I turn'd into a sty
And laid me down among the swine.

I See The Four-Fold Man

I see the Four-fold Man, The Humanity in deadly sleep
And its fallen Emanation, the Spectre and its cruel Shadow.
I see the Past, Present and Future existing all at once
Before me. O Divine Spirit, sustain me on thy wings,
That I may awake Albion from his long and cold repose;
For Bacon and Newton, sheath'd in dismal steel, their terrors hang
Like iron scourges over Albion: reasonings like vast serpents
Infold around my limbs, bruising my minute articulations.
I turn my eyes to the schools and universities of Europe
And there behold the Loom of Locke, whose Woof rages dire,
Wash'd by the Water-wheels of Newton: black the cloth
In heavy wreaths folds over every nation: cruel works
Of many Wheels I view, wheel without wheel, with cogs tyrannic
Moving by compulsion each other, not as those in Eden, which,
Wheel within wheel, in freedom revolve in harmony and peace.

If It Is True What
The Prophets Write

If it is true, what the Prophets write,
That the heathen gods are all stocks and stones,
Shall we, for the sake of being polite,
Feed them with the juice of our marrow-bones?
And if Bezaleel and Aholiab drew
What the finger of God pointed to their view,
Shall we suffer the Roman and Grecian rods
To compel us to worship them as gods?
They stole them from the temple of the Lord
And worshipp'd them that they might make inspirèd art abhorr'd;
The wood and stone were call'd the holy things,
And their sublime intent given to their kings.
All the atonements of Jehovah spurn'd,
And criminals to sacrifices turn'd.

Infant Joy

'I have no name;
I am but two days old.'
What shall I call thee?
'I happy am,
Joy is my name.'
Sweet joy befall thee!
Pretty joy!
Sweet joy, but two days old.
Sweet Joy I call thee:
Thou dost smile,
I sing the while;
Sweet joy befall thee!

Infant Sorrow

My mother groaned, my father wept,
Into the dangerous world I leapt;
Helpless, naked, piping loud,
Like a fiend hid in a cloud.
Struggling in my father's hands,
Striving against my swaddling bands,
Bound and weary, I thought best
To sulk upon my mother's breast.

Introduction To The Songs Of Innocence

Piping down the valleys wild,
Piping songs of pleasant glee,
On a cloud I saw a child,
And he laughing said to me:
'Pipe a song about a Lamb!'
So I piped with merry cheer.
'Piper, pipe that song again;'
So I piped: he wept to hear.
'Drop thy pipe, thy happy pipe;
Sing thy songs of happy cheer:!'
So I sang the same again,
While he wept with joy to hear.
'Piper, sit thee down and write
In a book, that all may read.'
So he vanish'd from my sight;
And I pluck'd a hollow reed,
And I made a rural pen,
And I stain'd the water clear,
And I wrote my happy songs
Every child may joy to hear.

Jerusalem

And did those feet in ancient time
Walk upon England's mountains green?
And was the holy Lamb of God
On England's pleasant pastures seen?
And did the Countenance Divine
Shine forth upon our clouded hills?
And was Jerusalem builded here
Among these dark Satanic mills?
Bring me my bow of burning gold:
Bring me my arrows of desire:
Bring me my spear: O clouds unfold!
Bring me my chariot of fire.
I will not cease from mental fight,
Nor shall my sword sleep in my hand
Till we have built Jerusalem
In England's green and pleasant land.

Jerusalem: England! Awake! Awake! Awake!

England! awake! awake! awake!
Jerusalem thy Sister calls!
Why wilt thou sleep the sleep of death
And close her from thy ancient walls?
Thy hills and valleys felt her feet
Gently upon their bosoms move:
Thy gates beheld sweet Zion's ways:
Then was a time of joy and love.
And now the time returns again:
Our souls exult, and London's towers
Receive the Lamb of God to dwell
In England's green and pleasant bowers.

Jerusalem: I See The Four-Fold Man, The Humanity In

Deadly Sleep
I see the Four-fold Man, The Humanity in deadly sleep
And its fallen Emanation, the Spectre and its cruel Shadow.
I see the Past, Present and Future existing all at once
Before me. O Divine Spirit, sustain me on thy wings,
That I may awake Albion from his long and cold repose;
For Bacon and Newton, sheath'd in dismal steel, their terrors hang
Like iron scourges over Albion: reasonings like vast serpents
Infold around my limbs, bruising my minute articulations.
I turn my eyes to the schools and universities of Europe
And there behold the Loom of Locke, whose Woof rages dire,
Wash'd by the Water-wheels of Newton: black the cloth
In heavy wreaths folds over every nation: cruel works
Of many Wheels I view, wheel without wheel, with cogs tyrannic
Moving by compulsion each other, not as those in Eden, which,
Wheel within wheel, in freedom revolve in harmony and peace.

Laughing Song

When the green woods laugh with the voice of joy,
And the dimpling stream runs laughing by;
When the air does laugh with our merry wit,
And the green hill laughs with the noise of it;
when the meadows laugh with lively green,
And the grasshopper laughs in the merry scene,
When Mary and Susan and Emily
With their sweet round mouths sing 'Ha, ha he!'
When the painted birds laugh in the shade,
Where our table with cherries and nuts is spread:
Come live, and be merry, and join with me,
To sing the sweet chorus of 'Ha, ha, he!'

London

I wandered through each chartered street,
Near where the chartered Thames does flow,
A mark in every face I meet,
Marks of weakness, marks of woe.
In every cry of every man,
In every infant's cry of fear,
In every voice, in every ban,
The mind-forged manacles I hear:
How the chimney-sweeper's cry
Every blackening church appals,
And the hapless soldier's sigh
Runs in blood down palace-walls.
But most, through midnight streets I hear
How the youthful harlot's curse
Blasts the new-born infant's tear,
And blights with plagues the marriage-hearse.

Love And Harmony

Love and harmony combine,
And round our souls entwine
While thy branches mix with mine,
And our roots together join.
Joys upon our branches sit,
Chirping loud and singing sweet;
Like gentle streams beneath our feet
Innocence and virtue meet.
Thou the golden fruit dost bear,
I am clad in flowers fair;
Thy sweet boughs perfume the air,
And the turtle buildeth there.
There she sits and feeds her young,
Sweet I hear her mournful song;
And thy lovely leaves among,
There is love, I hear his tongue.
There his charming nest doth lay,
There he sleeps the night away;
There he sports along the day,
And doth among our branches play.

Love's Secret

Never seek to tell thy love,
Love that never told can be;
For the gentle wind does move
Silently, invisibly.
I told my love, I told my love,
I told her all my heart;
Trembling, cold, in ghastly fears,
Ah! she did depart!
Soon as she was gone from me,
A traveler came by,
Silently, invisibly
He took her with a sigh.

Mad Song

The wild winds weep
And the night is a-cold;
Come hither, Sleep,
And my griefs infold:
But lo! the morning peeps
Over the eastern steeps,
And the rustling birds of dawn
The earth do scorn.
Lo! to the vault
Of paved heaven,
With sorrow fraught
My notes are driven:
They strike the ear of night,
Make weep the eyes of day;
They make mad the roaring winds,
And with tempests play.
Like a fiend in a cloud,
With howling woe,
After night I do crowd,
And with night will go;
I turn my back to the east,
From whence comforts have increas'd;
For light doth seize my brain
With frantic pain.

Milton: And Did Those Feet In Ancient Time

And did those feet in ancient time
Walk upon England's mountains green?
And was the holy Lamb of God
On England's pleasant pastures seen?
And did the Countenance Divine
Shine forth upon our clouded hills?
And was Jerusalem builded here
Among these dark Satanic mills?
Bring me my bow of burning gold:
Bring me my arrows of desire:
Bring me my spear: O clouds unfold!
Bring me my chariot of fire.
I will not cease from mental fight,
Nor shall my sword sleep in my hand
Till we have built Jerusalem
In England's green and pleasant land.

Milton: But In The Wine-Presses The Human Grapes

Sing Not Nor Dance

But in the Wine-presses the human grapes sing not nor dance:
They howl and writhe in shoals of torment, in fierce flames
consuming,
In chains of iron and in dungeons circled with ceaseless fires,
In pits and dens and shades of death, in shapes of torment and woe:
The plates and screws and racks and saws and cords and fires and
cisterns
The cruel joys of Luvah's Daughters, lacerating with knives
And whips their victims, and the deadly sport of Luvah's Sons.
They dance around the dying and they drink the howl and groan,
They catch the shrieks in cups of gold, they hand them to one
another:
These are the sports of love, and these the sweet delights of amorous
play,
Tears of the grape, the death sweat of the cluster, the last sigh
Of the mild youth who listens to the luring songs of Luvah.

Mock On, Mock On, Voltaire, Rousseau

Mock on, mock on, Voltaire, Rousseau;
Mock on, mock on; 'tis all in vain!
You throw the sand against the wind,
And the wind blows it back again.
And every sand becomes a gem
Reflected in the beams divine;
Blown back they blind the mocking eye,
But still in Israel's paths they shine.
The Atoms of Democritus
And Newton's Particles of Light
Are sands upon the Red Sea shore,
Where Israel's tents do shine so bright.

My Pretty Rose Tree

A flower was offered to me,
Such a flower as May never bore;
But I said 'I've a pretty rose tree,'
And I passed the sweet flower o'er.
Then I went to my pretty rose tree,
To tend her by day and by night;
But my rose turned away with jealousy,
And her thorns were my only delight.

My Spectre Around Me Night And Day

i

My spectre around me night and day
Like a wild beast guards my way;
My Emanation far within
Weeps incessantly for my sin.

ii

`A fathomless and boundless deep,
There we wander, there we weep;
On the hungry craving wind
My Spectre follows thee behind.

iii

`He scents thy footsteps in the snow,
Wheresoever thou dost go,
Thro' the wintry hail and rain.
When wilt thou return again?

iv

`Dost thou not in pride and scorn
Fill with tempests all my morn,
And with jealousies and fears
Fill my pleasant nights with tears?

v

`Seven of my sweet loves thy knife
Has bereavèd of their life.
Their marble tombs I built with tears,
And with cold and shuddering fears.

vi

`Seven more loves weep night and day
Round the tombs where my loves lay,

And seven more loves attend each night
Around my couch with torches bright.

vii

`And seven more loves in my bed

Crown with wine my mournful head,
Pitying and forgiving all
Thy transgressions great and small.
viii
`When wilt thou return and view
My loves, and them to life renew?
When wilt thou return and live?
When wilt thou pity as I forgive?'
a
`O'er my sins thou sit and moan:
Hast thou no sins of thy own?
O'er my sins thou sit and weep,
And lull thy own sins fast asleep.
b
`What transgressions I commit
Are for thy transgressions fit.
They thy harlots, thou their slave;
And my bed becomes their grave.
ix
`Never, never, I return:
Still for victory I burn.
Living, thee alone I'll have;
And when dead I'll be thy grave.
x
`Thro' the Heaven and Earth and Hell
Thou shalt never, never quell:

I will fly and thou pursue:
Night and morn the flight renew.'
c
`Poor, pale, pitiable form
That I follow in a storm;
Iron tears and groans of lead
Bind around my aching head.
xi
`Till I turn from Female love
And root up the Infernal Grove,

I shall never worthy be
To step into Eternity.
xii
`And, to end thy cruel mocks,
Annihilate thee on the rocks,
And another form create
To be subservient to my fate.
xiii
`Let us agree to give up love,
And root up the Infernal Grove;
Then shall we return and see
The worlds of happy Eternity.
xiv
`And throughout all Eternity
I forgive you, you forgive me.
As 1000 our dear Redeemer said:
"This the Wine, and this the Bread."'

Never Seek To Tell Thy Love

Never seek to tell thy love
Love that never told can be;
For the gentle wind does move
Silently, invisibly.
I told my love, I told my love,
I told her all my heart,
Trembling, cold, in ghastly fears--
Ah, she doth depart.
Soon as she was gone from me
A traveller came by
Silently, invisibly--
O, was no deny.

Night

The sun descending in the west,
The evening star does shine;
The birds are silent in their nest,
And I must seek for mine.
The moon, like a flower,
In heaven's high bower,
With silent delight
Sits and smiles on the night.
Farewell, green fields and happy groves,
Where flocks have took delight.
Where lambs have nibbled, silent moves
The feet of angels bright;
Unseen they pour blessing,
And joy without ceasing,
On each bud and blossom,
And each sleeping bosom.
They look in every thoughtless nest,
Where birds are covered warm;
They visit caves of every beast,
To keep them all from harm.
If they see any weeping
That should have been sleeping,
They pour sleep on their head,
And sit down by their bed.
When wolves and tigers howl for prey,
They pitying stand and weep;
Seeking to drive their thirst away,
And keep them from the sheep.
But if they rush dreadful,
The angels, most heedful,
Receive each mild spirit,
New worlds to inherit.
And there the lion's ruddy eyes

Shall flow with tears of gold,
And pitying the tender cries,

And walking round the fold,
Saying, 'Wrath, by His meekness,
And, by His health, sickness
Is driven away
From our immortal day.
'And now beside thee, bleating lamb,
I can lie down and sleep;
Or think on Him who bore thy name,
Graze after thee and weep.
For, washed in life's river,
My bright mane for ever
Shall shine like the gold
As I guard o'er the fold.'

Now Art Has Lost Its Mental Charms

`Now Art has lost its mental charms
France shall subdue the world in arms.'
So spoke an Angel at my birth;
Then said `Descend thou upon earth,
Renew the Arts on Britain's shore,
And France shall fall down and adore.
With works of art their armies meet
And War shall sink beneath thy feet.
But if thy nation Arts refuse,
And if they scorn the immortal Muse,
France shall the arts of peace restore
And save thee from the ungrateful shore.'
Spirit who lov'st Britannia's Isle
Round which the fiends of commerce smile --

Nurse's Song (Innocence)

When voices of children are heard on the green
And laughing is heard on the hill,
My heart is at rest within my breast
And everything else is still
Then come home my children the sun is gone down
And the dews of night arise
Come come leave off play, and let us away
Till the morning appears in the skies
No no let us play, for it is yet day
And we cannot go to sleep
Besides in the sky, the little birds fly
And the hills are all covered with sheep
Well well go & play till the light fades away
And then go home to bed
The little ones leaped & shouted & laugh'd
And all the hills echoed

On Another's Sorrow

Can I see another's woe,
And not be in sorrow too?
Can I see another's grief,
And not seek for kind relief?
Can I see a falling tear,
And not feel my sorrow's share?
Can a father see his child
Weep, nor be with sorrow filled?
Can a mother sit and hear
An infant groan, an infant fear?
No, no! never can it be!
Never, never can it be!
And can He who smiles on all
Hear the wren with sorrows small,
Hear the small bird's grief and care,
Hear the woes that infants bear --
And not sit beside the next,
Pouring pity in their breast,
And not sit the cradle near,
Weeping tear on infant's tear?
And not sit both night and day,
Wiping all our tears away?
Oh no! never can it be!
Never, never can it be!
He doth give his joy to all:
He becomes an infant small,
He becomes a man of woe,
He doth feel the sorrow too.
Think not thou canst sigh a sigh,
And thy Maker is not by:
Think not thou canst weep a tear,
And thy Maker is not year.

Oh He gives to us his joy,

That our grief He may destroy:
Till our grief is fled an gone
He doth sit by us and moan.

Preludium To Europe

The nameless shadowy female rose from out the breast of Orc,
Her snaky hair brandishing in the winds of Enitharmon;
And thus her voice arose:
'O mother Enitharmon, wilt thou bring forth other sons?
To cause my name to vanish, that my place may not be found,
For I am faint with travail,
Like the dark cloud disburden'd in the day of dismal thunder.
My roots are brandish'd in the heavens, my fruits in earth beneath
Surge, foam and labour into life, first born and first consum'd!
Consumed and consuming!
Then why shouldst thou, accursed mother, bring me into life?
I wrap my turban of thick clouds around my lab'ring head,
And fold the sheety waters as a mantle round my limbs;
Yet the red sun and moon
And all the overflowing stars rain down prolific pains.
Unwilling I look up to heaven, unwilling count the stars:
Sitting in fathomless abyss of my immortal shrine
I seize their burning power
And bring forth howling terrors, all devouring fiery kings,
Devouring and devoured, roaming on dark and desolate mountains,
In forests of eternal death, shrieking in hollow trees.
Ah mother Enitharmon!
Stamp not with solid form this vig'rous progeny of fires.
I bring forth from my teeming bosom myriads of flames,
And thou dost stamp them with a signet;
then they roam abroad
And leave me void as death.
Ah! I am drown'd in shady woe and visionary joy.
And who shall bind the infinite with an eternal band?
To compass it with swaddling bands?
and who shall cherish it
With milk and honey?
I see it smile, and I roll inward, and my voice is past.'

She ceased, and roll'd her shady clouds
Into the secret place.

Proverbs Of Hell (Excerpt From The Marriage Of

Heaven And H

In seed time learn, in harvest teach, in winter enjoy.

Drive your cart and your plow over the bones of the dead.

The road of excess leads to the palace of wisdom.

Prudence is a rich, ugly old maid courted by Incapacity.

He who desires but acts not, breeds pestilence.

The cut worm forgives the plow.

Dip him in the river who loves water.

A fool sees not the same tree that a wise man sees.

He whose face gives no light, shall never become a star.

Eternity is in love with the productions of time.

The busy bee has no time for sorrow.

The hours of folly are measur'd by the clock; but of wisdom, no clock can measure.

All wholesome food is caught without a net or a trap.

Bring out number, weight and measure in a year of dearth.

No bird soars too high, if he soars with his own wings.

A dead body revenges not injuries.

The most sublime act is to set another before you.

If the fool would persist in his folly he would become wise.

Folly is the cloak of knavery.

Shame is Pride's cloke.

Prisons are built with stones of law, brothels with bricks of religion.

The pride of the peacock is the glory of God.

The lust of the goat is the bounty of God.

The wrath of the lion is the wisdom of God.

The nakedness of woman is the work of God.

Excess of sorrow laughs. Excess of joy weeps.

The roaring of lions, the howling of wolves, the raging of the stormy sea, and the destructive sword, are portions of eternity, too great for the eye of man.

The fox condemns the trap, not himself.

Joys impregnate. Sorrows bring forth.
Let man wear the fell of the lion, woman the fleece of the sheep.
The bird a nest, the spider a web, man friendship.
The selfish, smiling fool, and the sullen, frowning
fool shall be both thought
wise, that they may be a rod.
What is now proved was once only imagin'd.
The rat, the mouse, the fox, the rabbit watch the roots; the lion, the
tyger, the horse, the elephant watch the fruits.
The cistern contains: the fountain overflows.
One thought fills immensity.
Always be ready to speak your mind, and a base man will avoid you.
Every thing possible to be believ'd is an image of truth.
The eagle never lost so much time as when he submitted
to learn of the crow.
The fox provides for himself, but God provides for the lion.
Think in the morning. Act in the noon. Eat in the evening. Sleep in
the night.
He who has suffer'd you to impose on him, knows you.
As the plow follows words, so God rewards prayers.
The tygers of wrath are wiser than the horses of instruction.
Expect poison from the standing water.
You never know what is enough unless
you know what is more than enough.
Listen to the fool's reproach! it is a kingly title!
The eyes of fire, the nostrils of air, the mouth
of water, the beard of earth.
The weak in courage is strong in cunning.
The apple tree never asks the beech how
he shall grow; nor the lion, the horse,
how he shall take his prey.
The thankful receiver bears a plentiful harvest.
If others had not been foolish, we should be so.
The soul of sweet delight can never be defil'd.
When thou seest an eagle, thou seest a portion
of genius; lift up thy head!
As the caterpiller chooses the fairest leaves to lay

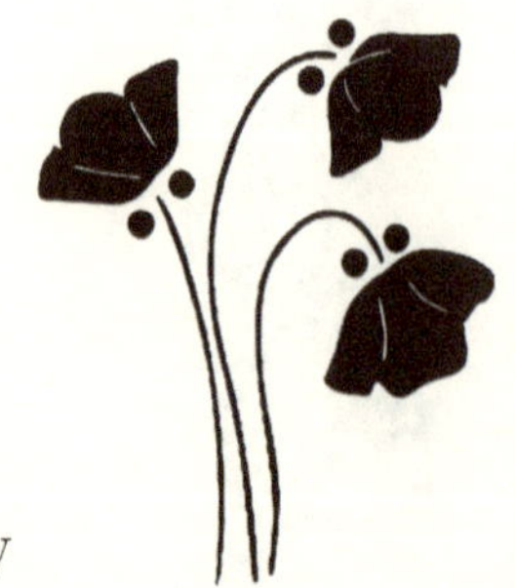

her eggs on, so the priest lays his curse on the fairest joys.
To create a little flower is the labour of ages.
Damn braces. Bless relaxes.
The best wine is the oldest, the best water the newest.
Prayers plow not! Praises reap not!
Joys laugh not! Sorrows weep not!
The head Sublime, the heart Pathos,
the genitals Beauty, the hands and feet Proportion.
As the air to a bird or the sea to a fish, so is contempt to the
contemptible.
The crow wish'd every thing was black, the owl that every thing was
white.
Exuberance is Beauty.
If the lion was advised by the fox, he would be cunning.
Improvement makes strait roads; but the crooked roads without
improvement
are roads of genius.
Sooner murder an infant in its cradle than nurse unacted desires.
Where man is not, nature is barren.
Truth can never be told so as to be understood, and not be believ'd.
Enough! or too much.

Reeds Of Innocence

Piping down the valleys wild,
Piping songs of pleasant glee,
On a cloud I saw a child,
And he laughing said to me:
'Pipe a song about a Lamb!'
So I piped with merry cheer.
'Piper, pipe that song again;'
So I piped: he wept to hear.
'Drop thy pipe, thy happy pipe;
Sing thy songs of happy cheer!'
So I sung the same again,
While he wept with joy to hear.
'Piper, sit thee down and write
In a book that all may read.'
So he vanish'd from my sight;
And I pluck'd a hollow reed,
And I made a rural pen,
And I stain'd the water clear,
And I wrote my happy songs
Every child may joy to hear.

Samson

Samson, the strongest of the children of men, I sing; how he was foiled by woman's arts, by a false wife brought to the gates of death! O Truth! that shinest with propitious beams, turning our earthly night to heavenly day, from presence of the Almighty Father, thou visitest our darkling world with blessed feet, bringing good news of Sin and Death destroyed! O whiterobed Angel, guide my timorous hand to write as on a lofty rock with iron pen the words of truth, that all who pass may read. -- Now Night, noontide of damned spirits, over the silent earth spreads her pavilion, while in dark council sat Philista's lords; and, where strength failed, black thoughts in ambush lay.

Their helmed youth and aged warriors in dust together lie, and Desolation spreads his wings over the land of Palestine: from side to side the land groans, her prowess lost, and seeks to hide her bruised head under the mists of night, breeding dark plots. For Dalila's fair arts have long been tried in vain; in vain she wept in many a treacherous tear.

`Go on, fair traitress; do thy guileful work; ere once again the changing moon her circuit hath performed, thou shalt overcome, and conquer him by force unconquerable, and wrest his secret from him.

Call thine alluring arts and honest-seeming brow, the holy kiss of love, and the transparent tear; put on fair linen that with the lily vies, purple and silver; neglect thy hair, to seem more lovely in thy loose attire; put on thy country's pride, deceit, and eyes of love decked in mild sorrow; and sell thy lord for gold.' For now, upon her sumptuous couch reclined in gorgeous pride, she still entreats, and still she grasps his vigorous knees with her fair arms. `Thou lov'st me not! thou'rt war, thou art not love! O foolish Dalila! O weak woman! it is death clothed in flesh thou lovest, and thou hast been encircled in his arms! Alas, my lord, what am I calling thee?

Thou art my God! To thee I pour my tears for sacrifice morning and evening. My days are covered with sorrow, shut up, darkened! By night I am deceived! Who says that thou wast born of mortal kind? Destruction was thy father, a lioness suckled thee, thy young hands tore human limbs, and gorged human flesh. Come hither, Death; art thou not Samson's servant? 'Tis Dalila that calls, thy master's wife; no, stay, and let thy master do the deed: one blow of that strong arm would ease my pain; then should I lay at quiet and have rest. Pity forsook thee at thy birth! O Dagon furious, and all ye gods of Palestine, withdraw your hand! I am but a weak woman. Alas, I am wedded to your enemy! I will go mad, and tear my crisped hair; 1000 I'll run about, and pierce the ears o' th' gods! O Samson, hold me not; thou lovest me not! Look not upon me with those deathful eyes!

Thou wouldst my death, and death approaches fast.' Thus, in false tears, she bath'd his feet, and thus she day by day oppressed his soul: he seemed a mountain; his brow among the clouds; she seemed a silver stream, his feet embracing. Dark thoughts rolled to and fro in his mind, like thunder clouds troubling the sky; his visage was troubled; his soul was distressed. `Though I should tell her all my heart, what can I fear? Though I should tell this secret of my birth, the utmost may be warded off as well when told as now.' She saw him moved, and thus resumes her wiles. `Samson, I'm thine; do with me what thou wilt: my friends are enemies; my life is death; I am a traitor to my nation, and despised; my joy is given into the hands of him who hates me, using deceit to the wife of his bosom. Thrice hast thou mocked me and grieved my soul. Didst thou not tell me with green withs to bind thy nervous arms; and, after that, when I had found thy falsehood, with new ropes to bind thee fast? I knew thou didst but mock me. Alas, when in thy sleep I bound thee with them to try thy truth, I cried, "The Philistines be upon thee, Samson!"

Then did suspicion wake thee; how didst thou rend the feeble ties! Thou fearest nought, what shouldst thou fear? Thy power is more than mortal, none can hurt thee; thy bones are brass, thy sinews are iron. Ten thousand spears are like the summer grass; an army of mighty men are as flocks in the valleys; what canst thou fear? I drink my tears like water; I live upon sorrow! O worse than wolves and tigers, what canst thou give when such a trifle is denied me? But O! at last thou mockest me, to shame my over-fond inquiry. Thou toldest me to weave thee to the beam by thy strong hair; I did even that to try thy truth; but, when I cried "The Philistines be upon thee!" then didst thou leave me to bewail that Samson loved me not.'

He sat, and inward griev'd; he saw and lov'd the beauteous suppliant, nor could conceal aught that might appease her; then, leaning on her bosom, thus he spoke: `Hear, O Dalila! doubt no more of Samson's love; for that fair breast was made the ivory palace of my inmost heart, where it shall lie at rest: for sorrow is the lot of all of woman born: for care was I brought forth, and labour is my lot: nor matchless might, nor wisdom, nor every gift enjoyed, can from the heart of man hide sorrow. Twice was my birth foretold from heaven, and twice a sacred vow enjoined me that I should drink no wine, nor eat of any unclean thing; for holy unto Israel's God I am, a Nazarite even from my mother's womb. Twice was it told, that it might not be broken. "Grant me a son, kind Heaven," Manoa cried; but Heaven refused. Childless he mourned, but thought his God knew best. In solitude, though not obscure, in Israel he lived, till venerable age came on: his flocks increased, and plenty crowned his board, beloved, revered of man. But God hath other joys in store. Is burdened Israel his grief? The son of his old age shall set it free!

The venerable sweetener of his life receives the promise first from Heaven. She saw the maidens play, and blessed their innocent mirth; she blessed each new-joined pair; but from her the long-wished deliverer shall spring. Pensive, alone she sat within the house, when busy day was fading, and calm evening, time for contemplation, rose from the forsaken east, and drew the curtains of heaven: pensive she sat, and thought on Israel's grief, and silent prayed to Israel's God; when lo! an angel from the fields of light entered the house. His form was manhood in the prime, and from his spacious brow shot terrors through the evening shade. But mild he hailed her, "Hail, highly favoured!" said he; "for lo! thou shalt conceive, and bear a son, and Israel's strength shall be upon his shoulders, and he shall be called Israel's Deliverer.

Now, therefore, drink no wine, and eat not any unclean thing, for he shall be a Nazarite to God." Then, as a nei 727 ghbour, when his evening tale is told, departs, his blessing leaving, so seemed he to depart: she wondered with exceeding joy, nor knew he was an angel. Manoa left his fields to sit in the house, and take his evening's rest from labour -- the sweetest time that God has allotted mortal man. He sat, and heard with joy, and praised God, who Israel still doth keep. The time rolled on, and Israel groaned oppressed. The sword was bright, while the ploughshare rusted, till hope grew feeble, and was ready to give place to doubting. Then prayed Manoa: "O Lord, thy flock is scattered on the hills! The wolf teareth them, Oppression stretches his rod over our land, our country is ploughed with swords, and reaped in blood. The echoes of slaughter reach from hill to hill. Instead of peaceful pipe the shepherd bears a sword, the ox-goad is turned into a spear. O when shall our Deliverer come? The Philistine riots on our flocks, our vintage is gathered by bands of enemies. Stretch forth thy hand, and save!" Thus prayed Manoa. The aged woman walked into the field, and lo! again the angel came, clad as a traveller fresh risen on his journey. She ran and called her husband, who came and talked with him. "O man of God," said he, "thou comest from far! Let us detain thee while I make ready a kid, that thou mayest sit and eat, and tell us of thy name and warfare; that, when thy sayings come to pass, we may honour thee." The Angel answered, "My name is Wonderful; inquire not after it, seeing it is a secret; but, if thou wilt, offer an offering unto the Lord.'"

Several Questions Answered

What is it men in women do require?
The lineaments of Gratified Desire.
What is it women do in men require?
The lineaments of Gratified Desire.
The look of love alarms
Because 'tis fill'd with fire;
But the look of soft deceit
Shall Win the lover's hire.
Soft Deceit & Idleness,
These are Beauty's sweetest dress.
He who binds to himself a joy
Dot the winged life destroy;
But he who kisses the joy as it flies
Lives in Eternity's sunrise.
Submitted by Josh Horn

Silent, Silent Night

Silent, silent night,
Quench the holy light
Of thy torches bright;
For possessed of Day
Thousand spirits stray
That sweet joys betray.
Why should joys be sweet
Used with deceit,
Nor with sorrows meet?
But an honest joy
Does itself destroy
For a harlot coy.

Sleep! Sleep! Beauty Bright

Sleep! sleep! beauty bright,
Dreaming o'er the joys of night;
Sleep! sleep! in thy sleep
Little sorrows sit and weep.
Sweet Babe, in thy face
Soft desires I can trace,
Secret joys and secret smiles,
Little pretty infant wiles.
As thy softest limbs I feel,
Smiles as of the morning steal
O'er thy cheek, and o'er thy breast
Where thy little heart does rest.
O! the cunning wiles that creep
In thy little heart asleep.
When thy little heart does wake
Then the dreadful lightnings break,
From thy cheek and from thy eye,
O'er the youthful harvests nigh.
Infant wiles and infant smiles
Heaven and Earth of peace beguiles.

Song

My silks and fine array,
My smiles and languish'd air,
By love are driv'n away;
And mournful lean Despair
Brings me yew to deck my grave;
Such end true lovers have.
His face is fair as heav'n
When springing buds unfold;
O why to him was't giv'n
Whose heart is wintry cold?
His breast is love's all-worshipp'd tomb,
Where all love's pilgrims come.
Bring me an axe and spade,
Bring me a winding sheet;
When I my grave have made
Let winds and tempests beat:
Then down I'll lie as cold as clay.
True love doth pass away!

Song: Memory, Hither Come

Memory, hither come,
And tune your merry notes;
And, while upon the wind
Your music floats,
I'll pore upon the stream
Where sighing lovers dream,
And fish for fancies as they pass
Within the watery glass.
I'll drink of the clear stream,
And hear the linnet's song;
And there I'll lie and dream
The day along:
And, when night comes, I'll go
To places fit for woe,
Walking along the darken'd valley
With silent Melancholy.

Songs Of Experience: Introduction

Hear the voice of the Bard!
Who Present, Past, & Future sees
Whose ears have heard
The Holy Word,
That walk'd among the ancient trees.
Calling the lapsed Soul
And weeping in the evening dew;
That might controll.
The starry pole;
And fallen fallen light renew!
O Earth O Earth return!
Arise from out the dewy grass;
Night is worn,
And the morn
Rises from the slumbrous mass.
Turn away no more:
Why wilt thou turn away
The starry floor
The watery shore
Is given thee till the break of day.

Songs Of Innocence: Introduction

Piping down the valleys wild
Piping songs of pleasant glee
On a cloud I saw a child.
And he laughing said to me.
Pipe a song about a Lamb:
So I piped with merry chear,
Piper, pipe that song again--
So I piped, he wept to hear.
Drop thy pipe thy happy pipe
Sing thy songs of happy chear,
So I sung the same again
While he wept with joy to hear
Piper sit thee down and write
In a book that all may read--
So he vanished from my sight
And I pluck'd a hollow reed.
And I made a rural pen,
And I stained the water clear,
And I wrote my happy songs,
Every child may joy to hear.

Spring

Sound the flute!
Now it's mute!
Bird's delight,
Day and night,
Nightingale,
In the dale,
Lark in sky,--
Merrily,
Merrily merrily, to welcome in the year.
Little boy,
Full of joy;
Little girl,
Sweet and small;
Cock does crow,
So do you;
Merry voice,
Infant noise;
Merrily, merrily, to welcome in the year.
Little lamb,
Here I am;
Come and lick
My white neck;
Let me pull
Your soft wool;
Let me kiss
Your soft face;
Merrily, merrily, to welcome in the year.

The Angel

I dreamt a dream! What can it mean?
And that I was a maiden Queen
Guarded by an Angel mild:
Witless woe was ne'er beguiled!
And I wept both night and day,
And he wiped my tears away;
And I wept both day and night,
And hid from him my heart's delight.
So he took his wings, and fled;
Then the morn blushed rosy red.
I dried my tears, and armed my fears
With ten-thousand shields and spears.
Soon my Angel came again;
I was armed, he came in vain;
For the time of youth was fled,
And grey hairs were on my head.

The Angel That Presided O'Er My Birth

The Angel that presided o'er my birth
Said, 'Little creature, form'd of Joy and Mirth,
'Go love without the help of any Thing on Earth.'

The Birds

He. Where thou dwellest, in what grove,
Tell me Fair One, tell me Love;
Where thou thy charming nest dost build,
O thou pride of every field!
She. Yonder stands a lonely tree,
There I live and mourn for thee;
Morning drinks my silent tear,
And evening winds my sorrow bear.
He. O thou summer's harmony,
I have liv'd and mourn'd for thee;
Each day I mourn along the wood,
And night hath heard my sorrows loud.
She. Dost thou truly long for me?
And am I thus sweet to thee?
Sorrow now is at an end,
O my Lover and my Friend!
He. Come, on wings of joy we'll fly
To where my bower hangs on high;
Come, and make thy calm retreat
Among green leaves and blossoms sweet.

The Blossom

Merry, merry sparrow!
Under leaves so green
A happy blossom
Sees you, swift as arrow,
Seek your cradle narrow,
Near my bosom.
Pretty, pretty robin!
Under leaves so green
A happy blossom
Hears you sobbing, sobbing,
Pretty, pretty robin,
Near my bosom.

The Book Of Thel
1 Does the Eagle know what is in the pit?
2 Or wilt thou go ask the Mole?
3 Can Wisdom be put in a silver rod?
4 Or Love in a golden bowl?

I

1.1 The daughters of the Seraphim led round their sunny flocks,
1.2 All but the youngest: she in paleness sought the secret air,
1.3 To fade away like morning beauty from her mortal day:
1.4 Down by the river of Adona her soft voice is heard,
1.5 And thus her gentle lamentation falls like morning dew:
1.6 'O life of this our spring! why fades the lotus of the water,
1.7 Why fade these children of the spring, born but to smile and fall?
1.8 Ah! Thel is like a wat'ry bow, and like a parting cloud;
1.9 Like a reflection in a glass; like shadows in the water;
1.10 Like dreams of infants, like a smile upon an infant's face;
1.11 Like the dove's voice; like transient day; like music in the air.
1.12 Ah! gentle may I lay me down, and gentle rest my head,
1.13 And gentle sleep the sleep of death, and gentle hear the voice
1.14 Of him that walketh in the garden in the evening time.'
1.15 The Lily of the valley, breathing in the humble grass,
1.16 Answer'd the lovely maid and said: 'I am a wat'ry weed,
1.17 And I am very small and love to dwell in lowly vales;
1.18 So weak, the gilded butterfly scarce perches on my head.
1.19 Yet I am visited from heaven, and he that smiles on all
1.20 Walks in the valley and each morn over me spreads his hand,
1.21 Saying, 'Rejoice, thou humble grass, thou new-born lily-flower,
1.22 Thou gentle maid of silent valleys and of modest brooks;
1.23 For thou shalt be clothed in light, and fed with morning manna,
1.24 Till summer's heat melts thee beside
the fountains and the springs
1.25 To flourish in eternal vales.' Then why should Thel complain?
1.26 Why should the mistress of the vales of Har utter a sigh?'
1.27 She ceas'd and smil'd in tears, then sat down in her silver shrine.
1.28 Thel answer'd: 'O thou little virgin of the peaceful valley,
1.29 Giving to those that cannot crave, the
voiceless, the o'ertired;

1.30 Thy breath doth nourish the innocent lamb,
he smells thy milky garments,
1.31 He crops thy flowers while thou sittest smiling in his face,
1.32 Wiping his mild and meekin mouth from all contagious taints.
1.33 Thy wine doth purify the golden honey; thy perfume,
1.34 Which thou dost scatter on every little blade of grass that
springs,
1.35 Revives the milked cow, and tames the fire-breathing steed.
1.36 But Thel is like a faint cloud kindled at the rising sun:
1.37 I vanish from my pearly throne, and who shall find my place?'
1.38 'Queen of the vales,' the Lily answer'd, 'ask the tender cloud,
1.39 And it shall tell thee why it glitters in the morning sky,
1.40 And why it scatters its bright beauty thro' the humid air.
1.41 Descend, O little Cloud, and hover before the eyes of Thel.'
1.42 The Cloud descended, and the Lily bow'd her modest head
1.43 And went to mind her numerous charge
among the verdant grass.

II

2.1 'O little Cloud,' the virgin said, 'I charge thee tell to me
2.2 Why thou complainest not when in one hour thou fade away:
2.3 Then we shall seek thee, but not find. Ah! Thel is like to thee:
2.4 I pass away: yet I complain, and no one hears my voice.'
2.5 The Cloud then shew'd his golden head
and his bright form emerg'd,
2.6 Hovering and glittering on the air before the face of Thel.
2.7 'O virgin, know'st thou not our steeds drink of the golden springs
2.8 Where Luvah doth renew his horses? Look'st thou on my youth,

2.9 And fearest thou, because I vanish and am seen no more,
2.10 Nothing remains? O maid, I tell thee, when I pass away
2.11 It is to tenfold life, to love, to peace and raptures holy:
2.12 Unseen descending, weigh my light wings upon balmy flowers,
2.13 And court the fair-eyed dew to take me to her shining tent:
2.14 The weeping virgin trembling kneels before the risen sun,
2.15 Till we arise link'd in a golden band and never part,
2.16 But walk united, bearing food to all our tender flowers.'
2.17 'Dost thou, O little Cloud? I fear that I am not like thee,
2.18 For I walk thro' the vales of Har, and smell the sweetest flowers,
2.19 But I feed not the little flowers; I hear the warbling birds,
2.20 But I feed not the warbling birds; they fly and seek their food:

2.21 But Thel delights in these no more, because I fade away;
2.22 And all shall say, 'Without a use this shining woman liv'd,
2.23 Or did she only live to be at death the food of worms?' '
2.24 The Cloud reclin'd upon his airy throne and answer'd thus:
2.25 'Then if thou art the food of worms, O virgin of the skies,
2.26 How great thy use, how great thy blessing! Every thing that lives
2.27 Lives not alone nor for itself. Fear not, and I will call
2.28 The weak worm from its lowly bed, and thou shalt hear its voice,
2.29 Come forth, worm of the silent valley, to thy pensive queen.'
2.30 The helpless worm arose, and sat upon the Lily's leaf,
2.31 And the bright Cloud sail'd on, to find his partner in the vale.

3.1 Then Thel astonish'd view'd the Worm upon its dewy bed.
3.2 'Art thou a Worm? Image of weakness, art thou but a Worm?
3.3 I see thee like an infant wrapped in the Lily's leaf
3.4 Ah! weep not, little voice, thou canst not speak, but thou canst
weep.
3.5 Is this a Worm? I see thee lay helpless and naked, weeping,
3.6 And none to answer, none to cherish thee with mother's smiles.'
3.7 The Clod of Clay heard the Worm's voice and rais'd her pitying
head:
3.8 She bow'd over the weeping infant, and her life exhal'd
3.9 In milky fondness: then on Thel she fix'd her humble eyes.
3.10 'O beauty of the vales of Har! we live not for ourselves.
3.11 Thou seest me the meanest thing, and so I am indeed.
3.12 My bosom of itself is cold, and of itself is dark;
3.13 But he, that loves the lowly, pours his oil upon my head,
3.14 And kisses me, and binds his nuptial bands around my breast,
3.15 And says: 'Thou mother of my children, I have loved thee
3.16 And I have given thee a crown that none can take away.'
3.17 But how this is, sweet maid, I know not, and I cannot know;
3.18 I ponder, and I cannot ponder; yet I live and love.'
3.19 The daughter of beauty wip'd her pitying tears with her white
veil,
3.20 And said: 'Alas! I knew not this, and therefore did I weep.
3.21 That God would love a Worm I knew, and punish the evil foot
3.22 That wilful bruis'd its helpless form; but that he cherish'd it

3.23 With milk and oil I never knew, and therefore did I weep;
3.24 And I complain'd in the mild air, because I fade away,
3.25 And lay me down in thy cold bed, and leave my shining lot.'
3.26 'Queen of the vales,' the matron Clay answer'd,
'I heard thy sighs,
3.27 And all thy moans flew o'er my roof, but
I have call'd them down.
3.28 Wilt thou, O Queen, enter my house? 'Tis given thee to enter
3.29 And to return: fear nothing, enter with thy virgin feet.'

IV

4.1 The eternal gates' terrific porter lifted the northern bar:
4.2 Thel enter'd in and saw the secrets of the land unknown.
4.3 She saw the couches of the dead, and where the fibrous roots
4.4 Of every heart on earth infixes deep its restless twists:
4.5 A land of sorrows and of tears where never smile was seen.
4.6 She wander'd in the land of clouds thro' valleys dark, list'ning
4.7 Dolours and lamentations; waiting oft beside a dewy grave
4.8 She stood in silence, list'ning to the voices of the ground,
4.9 Till to her own grave plot she came, and there she sat down,
4.10 And heard this voice of sorrow breathed from the hollow pit.
4.11 'Why cannot the Ear be closed to its own destruction?
4.12 Or the glist'ning Eye to the poison of a smile?
4.13 Why are Eyelids stor'd with arrows ready drawn,
4.14 Where a thousand fighting men in ambush lie?
4.15 Or an Eye of gifts and graces show'ring fruits and coined gold?
4.16 Why a Tongue impress'd with honey from every wind?
4.17 Why an Ear, a whirlpool fierce to draw creations in?
4.18 Why a Nostril wide inhaling terror, trembling, and affright?
4.19 Why a tender curb upon the youthful burning boy?
4.20 Why a little curtain of flesh on the bed
of our desire?'
4.21 The Virgin started from her seat, and
with a shriek
4.22 Fled back unhinder'd till she came into
the vales of Har.

The Book Of Urizen (Excerpts)

Lo, a shadow of horror is risen
In Eternity! Unknown, unprolific,
Self-clos'd, all-repelling: what demon
Hath form'd this abominable void,
This soul-shudd'ring vacuum? Some said
'It is Urizen.' But unknown, abstracted,
Brooding, secret, the dark power hid.
Times on times he divided and measur'd
Space by space in his ninefold darkness,
Unseen, unknown; changes appear'd
Like desolate mountains, rifted furious
By the black winds of perturbation.
For he strove in battles dire,
In unseen conflictions with shapes
Bred from his forsaken wilderness
Of beast, bird, fish, serpent and element,
Combustion, blast, vapour and cloud.
Dark, revolving in silent activity:
Unseen in tormenting passions:
An activity unknown and horrible,
A self-contemplating shadow,
In enormous labours occupied.
But Eternals beheld his vast forests;
Age on ages he lay, clos'd, unknown,
Brooding shut in the deep; all avoid
The petrific, abominable chaos.

His cold horrors silent, dark Urizen
Prepar'd; his ten thousands of thunders,
Rang'd in gloom'd array, stretch out across
The dread world; and the rolling of wheels,
As of swelling seas, sound in his clouds,
In his hills of stor'd snows, in his mountains

Of hail and ice; voices of terror
Are heard, like thunders of autumn
When the cloud blazes over the harvests

The Book Of Urizen: Chapter I

1. Lo, a shadow of horror is risen
In Eternity! Unknown, unprolific!
Self-closd, all-repelling: what Demon
Hath form'd this abominable void
This soul-shudd'ring vacuum?--Some said
"It is Urizen", But unknown, abstracted
Brooding secret, the dark power hid.
2. Times on times he divided, & measur'd
Space by space in his ninefold darkness
Unseen, unknown! changes appeard
In his desolate mountains rifted furious
By the black winds of perturbation
3. For he strove in battles dire
In unseen conflictions with shapes
Bred from his forsaken wilderness,
Of beast, bird, fish, serpent & element
Combustion, blast, vapour and cloud.
4. Dark revolving in silent activity:
Unseen in tormenting passions;
An activity unknown and horrible;
A self-contemplating shadow,
In enormous labours occupied
5. But Eternals beheld his vast forests
Age on ages he lay, clos'd, unknown
Brooding shut in the deep; all avoid
The petrific abominable chaos
6. His cold horrors silent, dark Urizen
Prepar'd: his ten thousands of thunders
Rang'd in gloom'd array stretch out across
The dread world, & the rolling of wheels
As of swelling seas, sound in his clouds
In his hills of stor'd snows, in his mountains
Of hail & ice; voices of terror,

Are heard, like thunders of autumn,

When the cloud blazes over the harvests

The Book Of Urizen: Chapter Ii

1. Earth was not: nor globes of attraction
The will of the Immortal expanded
Or contracted his all flexible senses.
Death was not, but eternal life sprung
2. The sound of a trumpet the heavens
Awoke & vast clouds of blood roll'd
Round the dim rocks of Urizen, so nam'd
That solitary one in Immensity
3. Shrill the trumpet: & myriads of Eternity,
Muster around the bleak desarts
Now fill'd with clouds, darkness & waters
That roll'd perplex'd labring & utter'd
Words articulate, bursting in thunders
That roll'd on the tops of his mountains
4. From the depths of dark solitude. From
The eternal abode in my holiness,
Hidden set apart in my stern counsels
Reserv'd for the days of futurity,
I have sought for a joy without pain,
For a solid without fluctuation
Why will you die O Eternals?
Why live in unquenchable burnings?
5. First I fought with the fire; consum'd
Inwards, into a deep world within:
A void immense, wild dark & deep,
Where nothing was: Natures wide womb
And self balanc'd stretch'd o'er the void
I alone, even I! the winds merciless
Bound; but condensing, in torrents
They fall & fall; strong I repell'd
The vast waves, & arose on the waters
A wide world of solid obstruction
6. Here alone I in books formd of metals

Have written the secrets of wisdom

The secrets of dark contemplation
By fightings and conflicts dire,
With terrible monsters Sin-bred:
Which the bosoms of all inhabit;
Seven deadly Sins of the soul.
7. Lo! I unfold my darkness: and on
This rock, place with strong hand the Book
Of eternal brass, written in my solitude.
8. Laws of peace, of love, of unity:
Of pity, compassion, forgiveness.
Let each chuse one habitation:
His ancient infinite mansion:
One command, one joy, one desire,
One curse, one weight, one measure
One King, one God, one Law.

The Book Of Urizen: Chapter Iii

1. The voice ended, they saw his pale visage
Emerge from the darkness; his hand
On the rock of eternity unclasping
The Book of brass. Rage siez'd the strong

2. Rage, fury, intense indignation
In cataracts of fire blood & gall
In whirlwinds of sulphurous smoke:
And enormous forms of energy;
All the seven deadly sins of the soul
In living creations appear'd
In the flames of eternal fury.

3. Sund'ring, dark'ning, thund'ring!
Rent away with a terrible crash
Eternity roll'd wide apart
Wide asunder rolling
Mountainous all around
Departing; departing; departing:
Leaving ruinous fragments of life
Hanging frowning cliffs & all between
An ocean of voidness unfathomable.

4. The roaring fires ran o'er the heav'ns
In whirlwinds & cataracts of blood
And o'er the dark desarts of Urizen
Fires pour thro' the void on all sides
On Urizens self-begotten armies.

5. But no light from the fires. all was darkness
In the flames of Eternal fury

6. In fierce anguish & quenchless flames
To the desarts and rocks He ran raging
To hide, but He could not: combining
He dug mountains & hills in vast strength,
He piled them in incessant labour,
In howlings & pangs & fierce madness

Long periods in burning fires labouring

Till hoary, and age-broke, and aged,
In despair and the shadows of death.
7. And a roof, vast petrific around,
On all sides He fram'd: like a womb;
Where thousands of rivers in veins
Of blood pour down the mountains to cool
The eternal fires beating without
From Eternals; & like a black globe
View'd by sons of Eternity, standing
On the shore of the infinite ocean
Like a human heart strugling & beating
The vast world of Urizen appear'd.
8. And Los round the dark globe of Urizen,
Kept watch for Eternals to confine,
The obscure separation alone;
For Eternity stood wide apart,
As the stars are apart from the earth
9. Los wept howling around the dark Demon:
And cursing his lot; for in anguish,
Urizen was rent from his side;
And a fathomless void for his feet;
And intense fires for his dwelling.
10. But Urizen laid in a stony sleep
Unorganiz'd, rent from Eternity
11. The Eternals said: What is this? Death
Urizen is a clod of clay.
12. Los howld in a dismal stupor,
Groaning! gnashing! groaning!
Till the wrenching apart was healed
13. But the wrenching of Urizen heal'd not
Cold, featureless, flesh or clay,
Rifted with direful changes
He lay in a dreamless night
14. Till Los rouz'd his fires, affrighted

At the formless unmeasurable death.

The Book Of Urizen: Chapter Iv

a

1. Los smitten with astonishment
Frightend at the hurtling bones
2. And at the surging sulphureous
Perturbed Immortal mad raging
3. In whirlwinds & pitch & nitre
Round the furious limbs of Los
4. And Los formed nets & gins
And threw the nets round about
5. He watch'd in shuddring fear
The dark changes & bound every change
With rivets of iron & brass;
6. And these were the changes of Urizen.

b.

1. Ages on ages roll'd over him!
In stony sleep ages roll'd over him!
Like a dark waste stretching chang'able
By earthquakes riv'n, belching sullen fires
On ages roll'd ages in ghastly
Sick torment; around him in whirlwinds
Of darkness the eternal Prophet howl'd
Beating still on his rivets of iron
Pouring sodor of iron; dividing
The horrible night into watches.
2. And Urizen (so his eternal name)
His prolific delight obscurd more & more
In dark secresy hiding in surgeing
Sulphureous fluid his phantasies.
The Eternal Prophet heavd the dark bellows,

And turn'd restless the tongs; and the hammer
Incessant beat; forging chains new & new
Numb'ring with links. hours, days & years

3. The eternal mind bounded began to roll
Eddies of wrath ceaseless round & round,
And the sulphureous foam surgeing thick
Settled, a lake, bright, & shining clear:
White as the snow on the mountains cold.
4. Forgetfulness, dumbness, necessity!
In chains of the mind locked up,
Like fetters of ice shrinking together
Disorganiz'd, rent from Eternity,
Los beat on his fetters of iron;
And heated his furnaces & pour'd
Iron sodor and sodor of brass
5. Restless turnd the immortal inchain'd
Heaving dolorous! anguish'd! unbearable
Till a roof shaggy wild inclos'd
In an orb, his fountain of thought.
6. In a horrible dreamful slumber;
Like the linked infernal chain;
A vast Spine writh'd in torment
Upon the winds; shooting pain'd
Ribs, like a bending cavern
And bones of solidness, froze
Over all his nerves of joy.
And a first Age passed over,
And a state of dismal woe.
7. From the caverns of his jointed Spine,
Down sunk with fright a red
Round globe hot burning deep
Deep down into the Abyss:
Panting: Conglobing, Trembling
Shooting out ten thousand branches
Around his solid bones.
And a second Age passed over,
And a state of dismal woe.

8. In harrowing fear rolling round;
His nervous brain shot branches

Round the branches of his heart.
On high into two little orbs
And fixed in two little caves
Hiding carefully from the wind,
His Eyes beheld the deep,
And a third Age passed over:
And a state of dismal woe.
9. The pangs of hope began,
In heavy pain striving, struggling.
Two Ears in close volutions.
From beneath his orbs of vision
Shot spiring out and petrified
As they grew. And a fourth Age passed
And a state of dismal woe.
10. In ghastly torment sick;
Hanging upon the wind;
Two Nostrils bent down to the deep.
And a fifth Age passed over;
And a state of dismal woe.
11. In ghastly torment sick;
Within his ribs bloated round,
A craving Hungry Cavern;
Thence arose his channeld Throat,
And like a red flame a Tongue
Of thirst & of hunger appeard.
And a sixth Age passed over:
And a state of dismal woe.
12. Enraged & stifled with torment
He threw his right Arm to the north
His left Arm to the south
Shooting out in anguish deep,
And his Feet stampd the nether Abyss
In trembling & howling & dismay.
And a seventh Age passed over:
And a state of dismal woe.

The Book Of Urizen: Chapter Ix

1. Then the Inhabitants of those Cities:
Felt their Nerves change into Marrow
And hardening Bones began
In swift diseases and torments,
In throbbings & shootings & grindings
Thro' all the coasts; till weaken'd
The Senses inward rush'd shrinking,
Beneath the dark net of infection.
2. Till the shrunken eyes clouded over
Discernd not the woven hipocrisy
But the streaky slime in their heavens
Brought together by narrowing perceptions
Appeard transparent air; for their eyes
Grew small like the eyes of a man
And in reptile forms shrinking together
Of seven feet stature they remain
3. Six days they shrunk up from existence
And on the seventh day they rested
And they bless'd the seventh day, in sick hope:
And forgot their eternal life
4. And their thirty cities divided
In form of a human heart
No more could they rise at will
In the infinite void, but bound down
To earth by their narrowing perceptions
They lived a period of years
Then left a noisom body
To the jaws of devouring darkness
5. And their children wept, & built
Tombs in the desolate places,
And form'd laws of prudence, and call'd them
The eternal laws of God
6. And the thirty cities remain

Surrounded by salt floods, now call'd

Africa: its name was then Egypt.
7. The remaining sons of Urizen
Beheld their brethren shrink together
Beneath the Net of Urizen;
Perswasion was in vain;
For the ears of the inhabitants,
Were wither'd, & deafen'd, & cold:
And their eyes could not discern,
Their brethren of other cities.
8. So Fuzon call'd all together
The remaining children of Urizen:
And they left the pendulous earth:
They called it Egypt, & left it.
9. And the salt ocean rolled englob'd.

The Book Of Urizen: Chapter V

1. In terrors Los shrunk from his task:
His great hammer fell from his hand:
His fires beheld, and sickening,
Hid their strong limbs in smoke.
For with noises ruinous loud;
With hurtlings & clashings & groans
The Immortal endur'd his chains,
Tho' bound in a deadly sleep.
2. All the myriads of Eternity:
All the wisdom & joy of life:
Roll like a sea around him,
Except what his little orbs
Of sight by degrees unfold.
3. And now his eternal life
Like a dream was obliterated
4. Shudd'ring, the Eternal Prophet smote
With a stroke, from his north to south region
The bellows & hammer are silent now
A nerveless silence, his prophetic voice
Siez'd; a cold solitude & dark void
The Eternal Prophet & Urizen clos'd
5. Ages on ages rolld over them
Cut off from life & light frozen
Into horrible forms of deformity
Los suffer'd his fires to decay
Then he look'd back with anxious desire
But the space undivided by existence
Struck horror into his soul.
6. Los wept obscur'd with mourning:
His bosom earthquak'd with sighs;
He saw Urizen deadly black,
In his chains bound, & Pity began,
7. In anguish dividing & dividing

For pity divides the soul
In pangs eternity on eternity
Life in cataracts pourd down his cliffs
The void shrunk the lymph into Nerves
Wand'ring wide on the bosom of night
And left a round globe of blood
Trembling upon the Void
Thus the Eternal Prophet was divided
Before the death-image of Urizen
For in changeable clouds and darkness
In a winterly night beneath,
The Abyss of Los stretch'd immense:
And now seen, now obscur'd, to the eyes
Of Eternals, the visions remote
Of the dark seperation appear'd.
As glasses discover Worlds
In the endless Abyss of space,
So the expanding eyes of Immortals
Beheld the dark visions of Los,
And the globe of life blood trembling
8. The globe of life blood trembled
Branching out into roots;
Fib'rous, writhing upon the winds;
Fibres of blood, milk and tears;
In pangs, eternity on eternity.
At length in tears & cries imbodied
A female form trembling and pale
Waves before his deathy face
9. All Eternity shudderd at sight
Of the first female now separate
Pale as a cloud of snow
Waving before the face of Los
10. Wonder, awe, fear, astonishment,
Petrify the eternal myriads;
At the first female form now separate
They call'd her Pity, and fled
11. "Spread a Tent, with strong curtains around them

"Let cords & stakes bind in the Void

That Eternals may no more behold them"
12. They began to weave curtains of darkness
They erected large pillars round the Void
With golden hooks fastend in the pillars
With infinite labour the Eternals
A woof wove, and called it Science

The Book Of Urizen: Chapter VI

1. But Los saw the Female & pitied
He embrac'd her, she wept, she refus'd
In perverse and cruel delight
She fled from his arms, yet he followd
2. Eternity shudder'd when they saw,
Man begetting his likeness,
On his own divided image.
3. A time passed over, the Eternals
Began to erect the tent;
When Enitharmon sick,
Felt a Worm within her womb.
4. Yet helpless it lay like a Worm
In the trembling womb
To be moulded into existence
5. All day the worm lay on her bosom
All night within her womb
The worm lay till it grew to a serpent
With dolorous hissings & poisons
Round Enitharmons loins folding,
6. Coild within Enitharmons womb
The serpent grew casting its scales,
With sharp pangs the hissings began
To change to a grating cry,
Many sorrows and dismal throes,
Many forms of fish, bird & beast,
Brought forth an Infant form
Where was a worm before.
7. The Eternals their tent finished
Alarm'd with these gloomy visions
When Enitharmon groaning
Produc'd a man Child to the light.
8. A shriek ran thro' Eternity:

And a paralytic stroke;

At the birth of the Human shadow.
9. Delving earth in his resistless way;
Howling, the Child with fierce flames
Issu'd from Enitharmon.
10. The Eternals, closed the tent
They beat down the stakes the cords
Stretch'd for a work of eternity;
No more Los beheld Eternity.
11. In his hands he seiz'd the infant
He bathed him in springs of sorrow
He gave him to Enitharmon.

The Book Of Urizen: Chapter Vii

1. They named the child Orc, he grew
   Fed with milk of Enitharmon
2. Los awoke her; O sorrow & pain!
   A tight'ning girdle grew,
   Around his bosom. In sobbings
   He burst the girdle in twain,
   But still another girdle
   Opressd his bosom, In sobbings
   Again he burst it. Again
   Another girdle succeeds
   The girdle was form'd by day;
   By night was burst in twain.
3. These falling down on the rock
   Into an iron Chain
   In each other link by link lock'd
4. They took Orc to the top of a mountain.
   O how Enitharmon wept!
   They chain'd his young limbs to the rock
   With the Chain of Jealousy
   Beneath Urizens deathful shadow
5. The dead heard the voice of the child
   And began to awake from sleep
   All things. heard the voice of the child
   And began to awake to life.
6. And Urizen craving with hunger
   Stung with the odours of Nature
   Explor'd his dens around
7. He form'd a line & a plummet
   To divide the Abyss beneath.
   He form'd a dividing rule:
8. He formed scales to weigh;
   He formed massy weights;
   He formed a brazen quadrant;

He formed golden compasses
And began to explore the Abyss
And he planted a garden of fruits
9. But Los encircled Enitharmon
With fires of Prophecy
From the sight of Urizen & Orc.
10. And she bore an enormous race

The Book Of Urizen: Chapter Viii

1. Urizen explor'd his dens
Mountain, moor, & wilderness,
With a globe of fire lighting his journey
A fearful journey, annoy'd
By cruel enormities: forms
Of life on his forsaken mountains
2. And his world teemd vast enormities
Frightning; faithless; fawning
Portions of life; similitudes
Of a foot, or a hand, or a head
Or a heart, or an eye, they swam mischevous
Dread terrors! delighting in blood
3. Most Urizen sicken'd to see
His eternal creations appear
Sons & daughters of sorrow on mountains
Weeping! wailing! first Thiriel appear'd
Astonish'd at his own existence
Like a man from a cloud born, & Utha
From the waters emerging, laments!
Grodna rent the deep earth howling
Amaz'd! his heavens immense cracks
Like the ground parch'd with heat; then Fuzon
Flam'd out! first begotten, last born.
All his eternal sons in like manner
His daughters from green herbs & cattle
From monsters, & worms of the pit.
4. He in darkness clos'd, view'd all his race,
And his soul sicken'd! he curs'd
Both sons & daughters; for he saw
That no flesh nor spirit could keep
His iron laws one moment.
5. For he saw that life liv'd upon death
The Ox in the slaughter house moans

The Dog at the wintry door
And he wept, & he called it Pity

And his tears flowed down on the winds
6. Cold he wander'd on high, over their cities
In weeping & pain & woe!
And where-ever he wanderd in sorrows
Upon the aged heavens
A cold shadow follow'd behind him
Like a spiders web, moist, cold, & dim
Drawing out from his sorrowing soul
The dungeon-like heaven dividing.
Where ever the footsteps of Urizen
Walk'd over the cities in sorrow.
7. Till a Web dark & cold, throughout all
The tormented element stretch'd
From the sorrows of Urizens soul
And the Web is a Female in embrio
None could break the Web, no wings of fire.
8. So twisted the cords, & so knotted
The meshes: twisted like to the human brain
9. And all calld it, The Net of Religion

The Book Of Urizen: Preludium

Of the primeval Priests assum'd power,
When Eternals spurn'd back his religion;
And gave him a place in the north,
Obscure, shadowy, void, solitary.
Eternals I hear your call gladly,
Dictate swift winged words, & fear not
To unfold your dark visions of torment.

The Caverns Of The Grave I've Seen

The Caverns of the Grave I've seen,
And these I show'd to England's Queen.
But now the Caves of Hell I view,
Who shall I dare to show them to?
What mighty soul i 362 n Beauty's form
Shall dauntless view the infernal storm?
Egremont's Countess can control
The flames of Hell that round me roll;
If she refuse, I still go on
Till the Heavens and Earth are gone,
Still admir'd by noble minds,
Follow'd by Envy on the winds,
Re-engrav'd time after time,
Ever in their youthful prime,
My designs unchang'd remain.
Time may rage, but rage in vain.
For above Time's troubled fountains,
On the great Atlantic Mountains,
In my Golden House on high,
There they shine eternally.

The Chimney Sweeper: A Little Black Thing Among

The Snow
A little black thing among the snow,
Crying 'weep! 'weep!' in notes of woe!
'Where are thy father and mother? say?'
'They are both gone up to the church to pray.
Because I was happy upon the heath,
And smil'd among the winter's snow,
They clothed me in the clothes of death,
And taught me to sing the notes of woe.
And because I am happy and dance and sing,
They think they have done me no injury,
And are gone to praise God and his Priest and King,
Who make up a heaven of our misery.'

The Chimney-Sweeper: When My Mother Died I Was

Very Young
When my mother died I was very young,
And my father sold me while yet my tongue
Could scarcely cry 'Weep! weep! weep! weep!'
So your chimneys I sweep, and in soot I sleep.
There's little Tom Dacre, who cried when his head,
That curled like a lamb's back, was shaved; so I said,
'Hush, Tom! never mind it, for, when your head's bare,
You know that the soot cannot spoil your white hair.'
And so he was quiet, and that very night,
As Tom was a-sleeping, he had such a sight! --
That thousands of sweepers, Dick, Joe, Ned, and Jack,
Were all of them locked up in coffins of black.
And by came an angel, who had a bright key,
And he opened the coffins, and let them all free;
Then down a green plain, leaping, laughing, they run,
And wash in a river, and shine in the sun.
Then naked and white, all their bags left behind,
They rise upon clouds, and sport in the wind;
And the Angel told Tom, if he'd be a good boy,
He'd have God for his father, and never want joy.
And so Tom awoke, and we rose in the dark,
And got with our bags and our brushes to work.
Though the morning was cold, Tom was happy and warm:
So, if all do their duty, they need not fear harm.

The Clod And The Pebble

'Love seeketh not itself to please,
Nor for itself hath any care,
But for another gives its ease,
And builds a heaven in hell's despair.'
So sung a little clod of clay,
Trodden with the cattle's feet;
But a pebble of the brook
Warbled out these meters meet:
'Love seeketh only Self to please,
To bind another to its delight,
Joys in another's loss of ease,
And builds a hell in heaven's despite.'

The Crystal Cabinet

The Maiden caught me in the wild,
Where I was dancing merrily;
She put me into her Cabinet,
And lock'd me up with a golden key.
This cabinet is form'd of gold
And pearl and crystal shining bright,
And within it opens into a world
And a little lovely moony night.
Another England there I saw
Another London with its Tower,
Another Thames and other hills,
And another pleasant Surrey bower.
Another Maiden like herself,
Translucent, lovely, shining clear,
Threefold each in the other clos'd
O, what a pleasant trembling fear!
O, what a smile! a threefold smile
Fill'd me, that like a flame I burn'd;
I bent to kiss the lovely Maid,
And found a threefold kiss return'd.
I strove to seize the inmost form
With ardor fierce and hands of flame,
But burst the Crystal Cabinet,
And like a weeping Babe became--
A weeping Babe upon the wild,
And weeping Woman pale reclin'd,
And in the outward air again,
I fill'd with woes the passing wind.

The Echoing Green

The sun does arise,
And make happy the skies;
The merry bells ring
To welcome the spring;
The skylark and thrush,
The birds of the bush,
Sing louder around
To the bell's cheerful sound,
While our sports shall be seen
On the Echoing Green.
Old John with white hair,
Does laugh away care,
Sitting under the oak,
Among the old folk.
They laugh at our play,
And soon they all say:
'Such, such were the joys
When we all, girls and boys,
In our youth time were seen
On the Echoing Green.'
Till the little ones, weary,
No more can be merry;
The sun does descend,
And our sports have an end.
Round the laps of their mothers
Many sisters and brother,
Like birds in their nest,
Are ready for rest,
And sport no more seen
On the darkening Green.

The Everlasting Gospel

The vision of Christ that thou dost see
Is my vision's greatest enemy.
Thine has a great hook nose like thine;
Mine has a snub nose like to mine.
Thine is the Friend of all Mankind;
Mine speaks in parables to the blind.
Thine loves the same world that mine hates;
Thy heaven doors are my hell gates.
Socrates taught what Meletus
Loath'd as a nation's bitterest curse,
And Caiaphas was in his own mind
A benefactor to mankind.
Both read the Bible day and night,
But thou read'st black where I read white.
Was Jesus gentle, or did He
Give any marks of gentility?
When twelve years old He ran away,
And left His parents in dismay.
When after three days' sorrow found,
Loud as Sinai's trumpet-sound:
'No earthly parents I confess—
My Heavenly Father's business!
Ye understand not what I say,
And, angry, force Me to obey.
Obedience is a duty then,
And favour gains with God and men.'
John from the wilderness loud cried;
Satan gloried in his pride.
'Come,' said Satan, 'come away,
I'll soon see if you'll obey!
John for disobedience bled,
But you can turn the stones to bread.
God's high king and God's high priest

Shall plant their glories in your breast,
If Caiaphas you will obey,
If Herod you with bloody prey
Feed with the sacrifice, and be
Obedient, fall down, worship me.'

Thunders and lightnings broke around,
And Jesus' voice in thunders' sound:
'Thus I seize the spiritual prey.
Ye smiters with disease, make way.
I come your King and God to seize,
Is God a smiter with disease?'
The God of this world rag'd in vain:
He bound old Satan in His chain,
And, bursting forth, His furious ire
Became a chariot of fire.
Throughout the land He took His course,
And trac'd diseases to their source.
He curs'd the Scribe and Pharisee,
Trampling down hypocrisy.
Where'er His chariot took its way,
There Gates of Death let in the Day,
Broke down from every chain and bar;
And Satan in His spiritual war
Dragg'd at His chariot-wheels: loud howl'd
The God of this world: louder roll'd
The chariot-wheels, and louder still
His voice was heard from Zion's Hill,
And in His hand the scourge shone bright;
He scourg'd the merchant Canaanite
From out the Temple of His Mind,
And in his body tight does bind
Satan and all his hellish crew;
And thus with wrath He did subdue
The serpent bulk of Nature's dross,
Till He had nail'd it to the Cross.
He took on sin in the Virgin's womb

And put it off on the Cross and tomb
To be worshipp'd by the Church of Rome.
Was Jesus humble? or did He
Give any proofs of humility?
Boast of high things with humble tone,
And give with charity a stone?
When but a child He ran away,
And left His parents in dismay.
When they had wander'd three days long
These were the words upon His tongue:

'No earthly parents I confess:
I am doing My Father's business.'
When the rich learnèd Pharisee
Came to consult Him secretly,
Upon his heart with iron pen
He wrote 'Ye must be born again.'
He was too proud to take a bribe;
He spoke with authority, not like a Scribe.
He says with most consummate art
'Follow Me, I am meek and lowly of heart,
As that is the only way to escape
The miser's net and the glutton's trap.'
What can be done with such desperate fools
Who follow after the heathen schools?
I was standing by when Jesus died;
What I call'd humility, they call'd pride.
He who loves his enemies betrays his friends.
This surely is not what Jesus intends;
But the sneaking pride of heroic schools,
And the Scribes' and Pharisees' virtuous rules;
For He acts with honest, triumphant pride,
And this is the cause that Jesus dies.
He did not die with Christian ease,
Asking pardon of His enemies:
If He had, Caiaphas would forgive;
Sneaking submission can always live.

He had only to say that God was the Devil,
And the Devil was God, like a Christian civil;
Mild Christian regrets to the Devil confess
For affronting him thrice in the wilderness;
He had soon been bloody Caesar's elf,
And at last he would have been Caesar himself,
Like Dr. Priestly and Bacon and Newton—
Poor spiritual knowledge is not worth a button
For thus the Gospel Sir Isaac confutes:
'God can only be known by His attributes;
And as for the indwelling of the Holy Ghost,
Or of Christ and His Father, it's all a boast
And pride, and vanity of the imagination,
That disdains to follow this world's fashion.'
To teach doubt and experiment
Certainly was not what Christ meant.

What was He doing all that time,
From twelve years old to manly prime?
Was He then idle, or the less
About His Father's business?
Or was His wisdom held in scorn
Before His wrath began to burn
In miracles throughout the land,
That quite unnerv'd the Seraph band?
If He had been Antichrist, Creeping Jesus,
He'd have done anything to please us;
Gone sneaking into synagogues,
And not us'd the Elders and Priests like dogs;
But humble as a lamb or ass
Obey'd Himself to Caiaphas.
God wants not man to humble himself:
That is the trick of the Ancient Elf.
This is the race that Jesus ran:
Humble to God, haughty to man,
Cursing the Rulers before the people
Even to the Temple's highest steeple,

And when He humbled Himself to God
Then descended the cruel rod.
'If Thou Humblest Thyself, Thou humblest Me.
Thou also dwell'st in Eternity.
Thou art a Man: God is no more:
Thy own Humanity learn to adore,
For that is My spirit of life.
Awake, arise to spiritual strife,
And Thy revenge abroad display
In terrors at the last Judgement Day.
God's mercy and long suffering
Is but the sinner to judgement to bring.
Thou on the Cross for them shalt pray—
And take revenge at the Last Day.'
Jesus replied, and thunders hurl'd:
'I never will pray for the world.
Once I did so when I pray'd in the Garden;
I wish'd to take with Me a bodily pardon.'
Can that which was of woman born,
In the absence of the morn,
When the Soul fell into sleep,
And Archangels round it weep,

Shooting out against the light
Fibres of a deadly night,
Reasoning upon its own dark fiction,
In doubt which is self-contradiction?
Humility is only doubt,
And does the sun and moon blot out,
Rooting over with thorns and stems
The buried soul and all its gems.
This life's five windows of the soul
Distorts the Heavens from pole to pole,
And leads you to believe a lie
When you see with, not thro', the eye
That was born in a night, to perish in a night,
When the soul slept in the beams of light.

Did Jesus teach doubt? or did He
Give any lessons of philosophy,
Charge Visionaries with deceiving,
Or call men wise for not believing?…
Was Jesus born of a Virgin pure
With narrow soul and looks demure?
If He intended to take on sin
The Mother should an harlot been,
Just such a one as Magdalen,
With seven devils in her pen.
Or were Jew virgins still more curs'd,
And more sucking devils nurs'd?
Or what was it which He took on
That He might bring salvation?
A body subject to be tempted,
From neither pain nor grief exempted;
Or such a body as might not feel
The passions that with sinners deal?
Yes, but they say He never fell.
Ask Caiaphas; for he can tell.—
'He mock'd the Sabbath, and He mock'd
The Sabbath's God, and He unlock'd
The evil spirits from their shrines,
And turn'd fishermen to divines;
O'erturn'd the tent of secret sins,
And its golden cords and pins,

In the bloody shrine of war
Pour'd around from star to star,—
Halls of justice, hating vice,
Where the Devil combs his lice.
He turn'd the devils into swine
That He might tempt the Jews to dine;
Since which, a pig has got a look
That for a Jew may be mistook.
"Obey your parents."—What says He?
"Woman, what have I to do with thee?

No earthly parents I confess:
I am doing my Father's business."
He scorn'd Earth's parents, scorn'd Earth's God,
And mock'd the one and the other's rod;
His seventy Disciples sent
Against Religion and Government—
They by the sword of Justice fell,
And Him their cruel murderer tell.
He left His father's trade to roam,
A wand'ring vagrant without home;
And thus He others' labour stole,
That He might live above control.
The publicans and harlots He
Selected for His company,
And from the adulteress turn'd away
God's righteous law, that lost its prey.'
Was Jesus chaste? or did He
Give any lessons of chastity?
The Morning blushèd fiery red:
Mary was found in adulterous bed;
Earth groan'd beneath, and Heaven above
Trembled at discovery of Love.
Jesus was sitting in Moses' chair.
They brought the trembling woman there.
Moses commands she be ston'd to death.
What was the sound of Jesus' breath?
He laid His hand on Moses' law;
The ancient Heavens, in silent awe,
Writ with curses from pole to pole,
All away began to roll.
The Earth trembling and naked lay
In secret bed of mortal clay;

On Sinai felt the Hand Divine
Pulling back the bloody shrine;
And she heard the breath of God,
As she heard by Eden's flood:

‘Good and Evil are no more!
Sinai’s trumpets cease to roar!
Cease, finger of God, to write!
The Heavens are not clean in Thy sight.
Thou art good, and Thou alone;
Nor may the sinner cast one stone.
To be good only, is to be
A God or else a Pharisee.
Thou Angel of the Presence Divine,
That didst create this Body of Mine,
Wherefore hast thou writ these laws
And created Hell’s dark jaws?
My Presence I will take from thee:
A cold leper thou shalt be.
Tho’ thou wast so pure and bright
That Heaven was impure in thy sight,
Tho’ thy oath turn’d Heaven pale,
Tho’ thy covenant built Hell’s jail,
Tho’ thou didst all to chaos roll
With the Serpent for its soul,
Still the breath Divine does move,
And the breath Divine is Love.
Mary, fear not! Let me see
The seven devils that torment thee.
Hide not from My sight thy sin,
That forgiveness thou may’st win.
Has no man condemnèd thee?’
‘No man, Lord.’ ‘Then what is he
Who shall accuse thee? Come ye forth,
Fallen fiends of heavenly birth,
That have forgot your ancient love,
And driven away my trembling Dove.
You shall bow before her feet;
You shall lick the dust for meat;
And tho’ you cannot love, but hate,
Shall be beggars at Love’s gate.
What was thy love? Let Me see it;

Was it love or dark deceit?'

'Love too long from me has fled;
'Twas dark deceit, to earn my bread;
'Twas covet, or 'twas custom, or
Some trifle not worth caring for;
That they may call a shame and sin
Love's temple that God dwelleth in,
And hide in secret hidden shrine
The naked Human Form Divine,
And render that a lawless thing
On which the Soul expands its wing.
But this, O Lord, this was my sin,
When first I let these devils in,
In dark pretence to chastity
Blaspheming Love, blaspheming Thee,
Thence rose secret adulteries,
And thence did covet also rise.
My sin Thou hast forgiven me;
Canst Thou forgive my blasphemy?
Canst Thou return to this dark hell,
And in my burning bosom dwell?
And canst Thou die that I may live?
And canst Thou pity and forgive?'
Then roll'd the shadowy Man away
From the limbs of Jesus, to make them His prey,
An ever devouring appetite,
Glittering with festering venoms bright;
Crying 'Crucify this cause of distress,
Who don't keep the secrets of holiness!
The mental powers by diseases we bind;
But He heals the deaf, the dumb, and the blind.
Whom God has afflicted for secret ends,
He comforts and heals and calls them friends.'
But, when Jesus was crucified,
Then was perfected His galling pride.
In three nights He devour'd His prey,

And still He devours the body of clay;
For dust and clay is the Serpent's meat,
Which never was made for Man to eat.
Seeing this False Christ, in fury and passion
I made my voice heard all over the nation.
What are those…

I am sure this Jesus will not do,
Either for Englishman or Jew.

The Fairy

'COME hither, my Sparrows,
My little arrows.
If a tear or a smile
Will a man beguile,
If an amorous delay
Clouds a sunshiny day,
If the step of a foot
Smites the heart to its root,
'Tis the marriage-ring...
Makes each fairy a king.'
So a Fairy sung.
From the leaves I sprung;
He leap'd from the spray
To flee away;
But in my hat caught,
He soon shall be taught.
Let him laugh, let him cry,
He's my Butterfly;
For I've pull'd out the sting
Of the marriage-ring.

The Fly

Little Fly,
Thy summer's play
My thoughtless hand
Has brushed away.
Am not I
A fly like thee?
Or art not thou
A man like me?
For I dance
And drink, and sing,
Till some blind hand
Shall brush my wing.
If thought is life
And strength and breath
And the want
Of thought is death;
Then am I
A happy fly,
If I live,
Or if I die.

The Four Zoas (Excerpt)

'What is the price of Experience? do men buy it for a song?
Or wisdom for a dance in the street? No, it is bought with the price
Of all that a man hath, his house, his wife, his children.
Wisdom is sold in the desolate market where none come to buy,
And in the wither'd field where the farmer plows for bread in vain.
It is an easy thing to triumph in the summer's sun
And in the vintage and to sing on the waggon loaded with corn.
It is an easy thing to talk of patience to the afflicted,
To speak the laws of prudence to the houseless wanderer,
To listen to the hungry raven's cry in wintry season
When the red blood is fill'd with wine and with the marrow of lambs.
It is an easy thing to laugh at wrathful elements,
To hear the dog howl at the wintry door, the ox in the slaughter
house moan;
To see a god on every wind and a blessing on every blast;
To hear sounds of love in the thunder storm that destroys our
enemies' house;
To rejoice in the blight that covers his field,
and the sickness that cuts off his children,
While our olive and vine sing and laugh round our door, and our
children bring fruits and flowers.
Then the groan and the dolor are quite forgotten, and the slave
grinding at the mill,
And the captive in chains, and the poor in the prison,
and the soldier in the field
When the shatter'd bone hath laid him groaning
among the happier dead.
It is an easy thing to rejoice in the
tents of prosperity:
Thus could I sing and thus rejoice: but it is
not so with me.'
'Compel the poor to live upon a crust of bread,
by soft mild arts.

Smile when they frown, frown when they smile; and when a man looks pale
With labour and abstinence, say he looks healthy and happy;
And when his children sicken, let them die; there are enough
Born, even too many, and our earth will be overrun
Without these arts. If you would make the poor live with temper,
With pomp give every crust of bread you give; with gracious cunning
Magnify small gifts; reduce the man to want a gift, and then give with pomp.
Say he smiles if you hear him sigh. If pale, say he is ruddy.

Preach temperance: say he is overgorg'd and drowns his wit
In strong drink, though you know that bread and water are all
He can afford. Flatter his wife, pity his children, till we can
Reduce all to our will, as spaniels are taught with art.'
The sun has left his blackness and has found a fresher morning,
And the mild moon rejoices in the clear and cloudless night,
And Man walks forth from midst of the fires: the evil is all consum'd.
His eyes behold the Angelic spheres arising night and day;
The stars consum'd like a lamp blown out, and in their stead, behold
The expanding eyes of Man behold the depths of wondrous worlds!
One Earth, one sea beneath; nor erring globes wander, but stars
Of fire rise up nightly from the ocean; and one sun
Each morning, like a new born man, issues with songs and joy
Calling the Plowman to his labour and the Shepherd to his rest.
He walks upon the Eternal Mountains, raising his heavenly voice,
Conversing with the animal forms of wisdom night and day,
That, risen from the sea of fire, renew'd walk o'er the Earth;

For Tharmas brought his flocks upon the hills, and in the vales
Around the Eternal Man's bright tent, the little children play
Among the woolly flocks. The hammer of Urthona sounds
In the deep caves beneath; his limbs renew'd, his Lions roar
Around the Furnaces and in evening sport upon the plains.
They raise their faces from the earth, conversing with the Man:
'How is it we have walk'd through fires and yet are not consum'd?
How is it that all things are chang'd, even as in ancient times?'

The French Revolution (Excerpt)

Thee the ancientest peer, Duke of Burgundy, rose from the
monarch's right hand, red as wines
From his mountains; an odor of war, like a ripe vineyard, rose from
his garments,
And the chamber became as a clouded sky; o'er the council he
stretch'd his red limbs,
Cloth'd in flames of crimson; as a ripe vineyard stretches over
sheaves of corn,
The fierce Duke hung over the council; around him crowd, weeping
in his burning robe,
A bright cloud of infant souls; his words fall like purple autumn on
the sheaves:
'Shall this marble built heaven become a clay cottage, this earth an
oak stool and these mowers
From the Atlantic mountains mow down all this great starry harvest
of six thousand years?
92 And shall Necker, the hind of Geneva, stretch out his crook'd
sickle o'er fertile France
93 Till our purple and crimson is faded to russet, and the kingdoms
of earth bound in sheaves,
94 And the ancient forests of chivalry hewn, and the joys of the
combat burnt for fuel;
95 Till the power and dominion is rent from the pole, sword and
sceptre from sun and moon,
96 The law and gospel from fire and air,
and eternal reason and science
97 From the deep and the solid, and man
lay his faded head down on the rock
98 Of eternity, where the eternal lion and
eagle remain to devour?
99 This to prevent--urg'd by cries in day,
and prophetic dreams hovering in

night,
100 To enrich the lean earth that craves, furrow'd with plows, whose seed is departing from her--
101 Thy nobles have gather'd thy starry hosts round this rebellious city,
102 To rouze up the ancient forests of Europe, with clarions of cloud breathing war,
103 To hear the horse neigh to the drum and trumpet, and the trumpet and war shout reply.
104 Stretch the hand that beckons the eagles of heaven; they cry over Paris, and wait
105 Till Fayette point his finger to Versailles; the eagles of heaven must have their prey!'
106 He ceas'd, and burn'd silent; red clouds roll round Necker; a weeping is heard o'er the palace.
107 Like a dark cloud Necker paus'd, and like thunder on the just man's burial day he paus'd;
108 Silent sit the winds, silent the meadows, while the husbandman and woman of weakness
109 And bright children look after him into the grave, and water his clay with love,
110 Then turn towards pensive fields; so Necker paus'd, and his visage was covered with clouds.
111 The King lean'd on his mountains, then lifted his head and look'd on his armies, that shone
112 Through heaven, tinging morning with beams of blood; then turning to Burgundy, troubled:
113 'Burgundy, thou wast born a lion! My soul is o'ergrown with distress.
114 For the nobles of France, and dark mists
roll round me and blot the writing of God
115 Written in my bosom. Necker rise! leave the
 kingdom, thy life is
surrounded with snares.
116 We have call'd an Assembly, but not to destroy;
 we have given gifts, not to the weak;
117 I hear rushing of muskets, and bright'ning of swords,

and visages redd'ningwith war,
118 Frowning and looking up from brooding villages and every
dark'ning city.
119 Ancient wonders frown over the kingdom, and cries of women
and babes are heard,
120 And tempests of doubt roll around me, and fierce sorrows,
because of the nobles of France.
121 Depart! answer not! for the tempest must fall, as in years that are
passed away.'
A wholly owned subsidiary of . Privacy Policy . AD

The Garden Of Love

I went to the Garden of Love,
And saw what I never had seen;
A Chapel was built in the midst,
Where I used to play on the green.
And the gates of this Chapel were shut
And 'Thou shalt not,' writ over the door;
So I turned to the Garden of Love
That so many sweet flowers bore.
And I saw it was filled with graves,
And tombstones where flowers should be;
And priests in black gowns were walking their rounds,
And binding with briars my joys and desires.

The Grey Monk

1 'I die, I die!' the Mother said,
2 'My children die for lack of bread.
3 What more has the merciless Tyrant said?'
4 The Monk sat down on the stony bed.
5 The blood red ran from the Grey Monk's side,
6 His hands and feet were wounded wide,
7 His body bent, his arms and knees
8 Like to the roots of ancient trees.
9 His eye was dry; no tear could flow:
10 A hollow groan first spoke his woe.
11 He trembled and shudder'd upon the bed;
12 At length with a feeble cry he said:
13 'When God commanded this hand to write
14 In the studious hours of deep midnight,
15 He told me the writing I wrote should prove
16 The bane of all that on Earth I lov'd.
17 My Brother starv'd between two walls,
18 His Children's cry my soul appalls;
19 I mock'd at the rack and griding chain,
20 My bent body mocks their torturing pain.
21 Thy father drew his sword in the North,
22 With his thousands strong he marched forth;
23 Thy Brother has arm'd himself in steel
24 To avenge the wrongs thy Children feel.
25 But vain the Sword and vain the Bow,
26 They never can work War's overthrow.
27 The Hermit's prayer and the Widow's tear
28 Alone can free the World from fear.
29 For a Tear is an intellectual thing,
30 And a Sigh is the sword of an Angel King,
31 And the bitter groan of the Martyr's woe
32 Is an arrow from the Almighty's bow.
33 The hand of Vengeance found the bed

34 To which the Purple Tyrant fled;
35 The iron hand crush'd the Tyrant's head
36 And became a Tyrant in his stead.'

The Human Abstract

Pity would be no more
If we did not make somebody Poor;
And Mercy no more could be
If all were as happy as we.
And mutual fear brings peace,
Till the selfish loves increase:
Then Cruelty knits a snare,
And spreads his baits with care.
He sits down with holy fears,
And waters the grounds with tears;
Then Humility takes its root
Underneath his foot.
Soon spreads the dismal shade
Of Mystery over his head;
And the Catterpiller and Fly
Feed on the Mystery.
And it bears the fruit of Deceit,
Ruddy and sweet to eat;
And the Raven his nest has made
In its thickest shade.
The Gods of the earth and sea
Sought thro' Nature to find this Tree;
But their search was all in vain:
There grows one in the Human Brain.

The Invocation

Daughters of Beulah! Muses who inspire the Poet's Song,
Record the journey of immortal Milton thro' your realms
Of terror and mild moony lustre, in soft Sexual delusions
Of varièd beauty, to delight the wanderer, and repose
His burning thirst and freezing hunger! Come into my hand,
By your mild power descending down the nerves of my right arm
From out the portals of my Brain, where by your ministry
The Eternal Great Humanity Divine planted His Paradise,
And in it caus'd the Spectres of the Dead to take sweet form
In likeness of Himself. Tell also of the False Tongue, vegetated
Beneath your land of Shadows, of its sacrifices and
Its offerings; even till Jesus, the image of the Invisible God,
Became its prey; a curse, an offering, and an atonement
For Death Eternal, in the Heavens of Albion, and before the Gates
Of Jerusalem his Emanation, in the Heavens beneath Beulah!

The Lamb

Little Lamb, who made thee?
Dost thou know who made thee?
Gave thee life, and bid thee feed,
By the stream and o'er the mead;
Gave thee clothing of delight,
Softest clothing, woolly, bright;
Gave thee such a tender voice,
Making all the vales rejoice?
Little Lamb, who made thee?
Dost thou know who made thee?
Little Lamb, I'll tell thee,
Little Lamb, I'll tell thee.
He is called by thy name,
For He calls Himself a Lamb.
He is meek, and He is mild;
He became a little child.
I a child, and thou a lamb,
We are called by His name.
Little Lamb, God bless thee!
Little Lamb, God bless thee!

The Land Of Dreams

Awake, awake, my little boy!
Thou wast thy mother's only joy;
Why dost thou weep in thy gentle sleep?
Awake! thy father does thee keep.
'O, what land is the Land of Dreams?
What are its mountains, and what are its streams?
O father! I saw my mother there,
Among the lilies by waters fair.
'Among the lambs, cloth? d in white,
She walk'd with her Thomas in sweet delight.
I wept for joy, like a dove I mourn;
O! when shall I again return? '
Dear child, I also by pleasant streams
Have wander'd all night in the Land of Dreams;
But tho' calm and warm the waters wide,
I could not get to the other side.
'Father, O father! what do we here
In this land of unbelief and fear?
The Land of Dreams is better far
Above the light of the morning star.'

The Lily

The modest Rose puts forth a thorn,
The humble sheep a threat'ning horn:
While the Lily white shall in love delight,
Nor a thorn nor a threat stain her beauty bright.

The Little Black Boy

My mother bore me in the southern wild,
And I am black, but oh my soul is white!
White as an angel is the English child,
But I am black, as if bereaved of light.
My mother taught me underneath a tree,
And, sitting down before the heat of day,
She took me on her lap and kissed me,
And, pointed to the east, began to say:
'Look on the rising sun: there God does live,
And gives His light, and gives His heat away,
And flowers and trees and beasts and men receive
Comfort in morning, joy in the noonday.
'And we are put on earth a little space,
That we may learn to bear the beams of love
And these black bodies and this sunburnt face
Is but a cloud, and like a shady grove.
'For when our souls have learn'd the heat to bear,
The cloud will vanish, we shall hear His voice,
Saying, 'Come out from the grove, my love and care
And round my golden tent like lambs rejoice','
Thus did my mother say, and kissed me;
And thus I say to little English boy.
When I from black and he from white cloud free,
And round the tent of God like lambs we joy
I'll shade him from the heat till he can bear
To lean in joy upon our Father's knee;
And then I'll stand and stroke his silver hair,
And be like him, and he will then love me.

The Little Boy Found

The little boy lost in the lonely fen,
Led by the wandering light,
Began to cry, but God, ever nigh,
Appeared like his father, in white.
He kissed the child, and by the hand led,
And to his mother brought,
Who in sorrow pale, through the lonely dale,
The little boy weeping sought.

The Little Boy Lost

'Father, father, where are you going?
Oh do not walk so fast!
Speak, father, speak to you little boy,
Or else I shall be lost.'
The night was dark, no father was there,
The child was wet with dew;
The mire was deep, and the child did weep,
And away the vapour flew.

The Little Girl Found

All the night in woe,
Lyca's parents go:
Over vallies deep.
While the desarts weep.
Tired and woe-begone.
Hoarse with making moan:
Arm in arm seven days.
They trac'd the desert ways.
Seven nights they sleep.
Among shadows deep:
And dream they see their child
Starvdd in desert wild.
Pale thro' pathless ways
The fancied image strays.
Famish'd, weeping, weak
With hollow piteous shriek
Rising from unrest,
The trembling woman prest,
With feet of weary woe;
She could no further go.
In his arms he bore.
Her arm'd with sorrow sore:
Till before their way
A couching lion lay.
Turning back was vain,
Soon his heavy mane.
Bore them to the ground;
Then he stalk'd around.
Smelling to his prey,
But their fears allay,
When he licks their hands:
And silent by them stands.

They look upon his eyes

Fill'd with deep surprise:
And wondering behold.
A spirit arm'd in gold.
On his head a crown
On his shoulders down,
Flow'd his golden hair.
Gone was all their care.
Follow me he said,
Weep not for the maid;
In my palace deep.
Lyca lies asleep.
Then they followed,
Where the vision led;
And saw their sleeping child,
Among tygers wild.
To this day they dwell
In a lonely dell
Nor fear the wolvish howl,
Nor the lion's growl.

The Little Girl Lost

In futurity
I prophesy see.
That the earth from sleep.
(Grave the sentence deep)
Shall arise and seek
For her maker meek:
And the desart wild
Become a garden mild.
In the southern clime,
Where the summers prime
Never fades away;
Lovely Lyca lay.
Seven summers old
Lovely Lyca told,
She had wandered long.
Hearing wild birds song.
Sweet sleep come to me
Underneath this tree;
Do father, mother weep.--
"Where can Lyca sleep".
Lost in desert wild
Is your little child.
How can Lyca sleep.
If her mother weep.
If her heart does ake.
Then let Lyca wake;
If my mother sleep,
Lyca shall not weep.
Frowning, frowning night,
O'er this desert bright.
Let thy moon arise.
While I close my eyes.

Sleeping Lyca lay:

While the beasts of prey,
Come from caverns deep,
View'd the maid asleep
The kingly lion stood
And the virgin view'd:
Then he gambolled round
O'er the hallowed ground:
Leopards, tygers play,
Round her as she lay;
While the lion old,
Bow'd his mane of gold,
And her bosom lick,
And upon her neck,
From his eyes of flame,
Ruby tears there came;
While the lioness
Loos'd her slender dress,
And naked they convey'd
To caves the sleeping maid.

The Little Vagabond

Dear mother, dear mother, the church is cold,
But the ale-house is healthy and pleasant and warm;
Besides I can tell where I am used well,
Such usage in Heaven will never do well.
But if at the church they would give us some ale,
And a pleasant fire our souls to regale,
We'd sing and we'd pray all the live-long day,
Nor ever once wish from the church to stray.
Then the parson might preach, and drink, and sing,
And we'd be as happy as birds in the spring;
And modest Dame Lurch, who is always at church,
Would not have bandy children, nor fasting, nor birch.
And God, like a father rejoicing to see
His children as pleasant and happy as he,
Would have no more quarrel with the Devil or the barrel,
But kiss him, and give him both drink and apparel.

The New Jerusalem

And did those feet in ancient time
      Walk upon England's mountains green?
      And was the holy Lamb of God
      On England's pleasant pastures seen?
      And did the Countenance Divine
      Shine forth upon our clouded hills?
      And was Jerusalem builded here
      Among these dark Satanic Mills?
      Bring me my bow of burning gold!
      Bring me my arrows of desire!
      Bring me my spear! O clouds, unfold!
      Bring me my charriot of fire!
      I will not cease from mental fight,
      Nor shall my sword sleep in my hand
      Till we have built Jerusalem
      In England's green and pleasant land.

The Question Answered

What is it men in women do require?
The lineaments of gratified Desire.
What is it women do in men require?
The lineaments of gratified Desire

The Rhine Was Red.

The Rhine was red with humane blood,
The Danube roll'd a purple tide,
On the Euphrates Satan stood
And over Asia stretch'd his pride.
He wither'd up sweet Zion's Hill
From every Nation of the Earth;
He wither'd up Jerusalem's Gates
And in a dark Land gave her birth.
He wither'd up the Human Form
By laws of sacrifice for sin,
Till it became a Mortal Worm,
But O! translucent all within.
Spectre of Albion! warlike Fiend!
In clouds of blood and ruin roll'd,
I here reclaim thee as my own,
My Selfhood! Satan! arm'd in gold.
Is this thy soft Family-Love,
Thy cruel Patriarchal pride,
Planting the Family alone,
Destroying all the World beside?
A man's worst enemies are those
Of his own house and family;
And he who makes his law a curse,
By his own law shall surely die.
In my Exchanges every Land,
Shall walk, and mine in every Land,
Mutual shall build Jerusalem,
Both heart in heart and hand in hand.

The Schoolboy

I love to rise in a summer morn
When the birds sing on every tree;
The distant huntsman winds his horn,
And the skylark sings with me.
O! what sweet company!
But to go to school on a summer morn,
O! it drives all joy away;
Under a cruel eye outworn,
The little ones spend the day
In sighing and dismay.
Ah! then at times I drooping sit,
And spend many an anxious hour,
Nor in my book can I take delight,
Nor sit in learning's bower,
Worn thro' with the dreary shower.
How can the bird that is born for joy
Sit in a cage and sing?
How can a child, when fears annoy,
But droop his tender wing,
And forget his youthful spring?
O! father and mother, if buds are nipped
And blossoms blown away,
And if the tender plants are stripped
Of their joy in the springing day,
By sorrow and care's dismay,
How shall the summer arise in joy,
Or the summer's fruits appear?
Or how shall we gather what griefs destroy,
Or bless the mellowing year,
When the blasts of winter appear?

The Shepherd

How sweet is the shepherd's sweet lot!
From the morn to the evening he strays;
He shall follow his sheep all the day,
And his tongue shall be filled with praise.
For he hears the lambs' innocent call,
And he hears the ewes' tender reply;
He is watchful while they are in peace,
For they know when their shepherd is nigh.

The Sick Rose

O Rose, thou art sick!
The invisible worm
That flies in the night,
In the howling storm,
Has found out thy bed
Of crimson joy:
And his dark secret love
Does thy life destroy.

The Sky Is An Immortal Tent Built By The Sons Of Los

The sky is an immortal tent built by the Sons of Los:
And every space that a man views around his dwelling-place
Standing on his own roof or in his garden on a mount
Of twenty-five cubits in height, such space is his universe:
And on its verge the sun rises and sets, the clouds bow
To meet the flat earth and the sea in such an order'd space:
The starry heavens reach no further, but here bend and set
On all sides, and the two Poles turn on their valves of gold:
And if he moves his dwelling-place, his heavens also move
Where'er he goes, and all his neighbourhood bewail his loss.
Such are the spaces called Earth and such its dimension.
As to that false appearance which appears to the reasoner
As of a globe rolling through voidness, it is a delusion of Ulro.
The microscope knows not of this nor the telescope: they alter
The ratio of the spectator's organs, but leave objects untouch'd.
For every space larger than a red globule of Man's blood
Is visionary, and is created by the Hammer of Los;
And every space smaller than a globule of Man's blood opens
Into Eternity of which this vegetable Earth is but a shadow.
The red globule is the unwearied sun by Los created
To measure time and space to mortal men every morning.

The Smile

There is a Smile of Love
And there is a Smile of Deceit
And there is a Smile of Smiles
In which these two Smiles meet
And there is a Frown of Hate
And there is a Frown of disdain
And there is a Frown of Frowns
Which you strive to forget in vain
For it sticks in the Hearts deep Core
And it sticks in the deep Back bone
And no Smile that ever was smild
But only one Smile alone
That betwixt the Cradle & Grave
It only once Smild can be
But when it once is Smild
Theres an end to all Misery

The Song Of Los   AFRICA

I will sing you a song of Los. the Eternal Prophet:
He sung it to four harps at the tables of Eternity.
In heart-formed Africa.
Urizen faded! Ariston shudderd!
And thus the Song began

Adam stood in the garden of Eden:
And Noah on the mountains of Ararat;
They saw Urizen give his Laws to the Nations
By the hands of the children of Los.

Adam shudderd! Noah faded! black grew the sunny African
When Rintrah gave Abstract Philosophy to Brama in the East:
(Night spoke to the Cloud!
Lo these Human form'd spirits in smiling hipocrisy. War
Against one another; so let them War on; slaves to the eternal
Elements)
Noah shrunk, beneath the waters;
Abram fled in fires from Chaldea;
Moses beheld upon Mount Sinai forms of dark delusion:

To Trismegistus. Palamabron gave an abstract Law:
To Pythagoras Socrates & Plato.

Times rolled on o'er all the sons of Har, time after time
Orc on Mount Atlas howld, chain'd down with the Chain of Jealousy
Then Oothoon hoverd over Judah & Jerusalem
And Jesus heard her voice (a man of sorrows) he recievd
A Gospel from wretched Theotormon.

The human race began to wither, for the healthy built
Secluded places, fearing the joys of Love
And the disease'd only propagated:
So Antamon call'd up Leutha from
her valleys of delight:
And to Mahomet a loose Bible gave.
But in the North, to Odin, Sotha gave a Code of War,
Because of Diralada thinking to reclaim his joy.

These were the Churches: Hospitals: Castles: Palaces:
Like nets & gins & traps to catch the joys of Eternity
And all the rest a desart;
Till like a dream Eternity was obliterated & erased.
Since that dread day when Har and Heva fled.
Because their brethren & sisters liv'd in War & Lust;
And as they fled they shrunk
Into two narrow doleful forms:
Creeping in reptile flesh upon
The bosom of the ground:
And all the vast of Nature shrunk
Before their shrunken eyes.
Thus the terrible race of Los & Enitharmon gave
Laws & Religions to the sons of Har binding them more
And more to Earth: closing and restraining:
Till a Philosophy of Five Senses was complete
Urizen wept & gave it into the hands of Newton & Locke
Clouds roll heavy upon the Alps round Rousseau & Voltaire:
And on the mountains of Lebanon round the deceased Gods
Of Asia; & on the deserts of Africa round the Fallen Angels
The Guardian Prince of Albion burns in his nightly tent

ASIA

The Kings of Asia heard
The howl rise up from Europe!
And each ran out from his Web;
From his ancient woven Den;
For the darkness of Asia was startled
At the thick-flaming, thought-creating fires of Orc.
And the Kings of Asia stood
And cried in bitterness of soul.
Shall not the King call for Famine from the heath?
Nor the Priest, for Pestilence from the fen?
To restrain! to dismay! to thin!
The inhabitants of mountain and plain;

In the day, of full-feeding prosperity;
And the night of delicious songs.

Shall not the Councellor throw his curb
Of Poverty on the laborious?
To fix the price of labour;
To invent allegoric riches:
And the privy admonishers of men
Call for fires in the City
For heaps of smoking ruins,
In the night of prosperity & wantonness
To turn man from his path,
To restrain the child from the womb,
To cut off the bread from the city,
That the remnant may learn to obey.
That the pride of the heart may fail;
That the lust of the eyes may be quench'd:
That the delicate ear in its infancy
May be dull'd; and the nostrils clos'd up;
To teach mortal worms the path
That leads from the gates of the Grave.
Urizen heard them cry!
And his shudd'ring waving wings
Went enormous above the red flames
Drawing clouds of despair thro' the heavens
Of Europe as he went:
And his Books of brass iron & gold
Melted over the land as he flew,
Heavy-waving, howling, weeping.
And he stood over Judea:
And stay'd in his ancient place:
And stretch'd his clouds over Jerusalem;
For Adam, a mouldering skeleton
Lay bleach'd on the garden of Eden;

And Noah as white as snow
On the mountains of Ararat.
Then the thunders of Urizen bellow'd aloud
From his woven darkness above.
Orc raging in European darkness
Arose like a pillar of fire above the Alps

Like a serpent of fiery flame!
The sullen Earth
Shrunk!
Forth from the dead dust rattling bones to bones
Join: shaking convuls'd the shivring clay breathes
And all flesh naked stands: Fathers and Friends;
Mothers & Infants; Kings & Warriors:
The Grave shrieks with delight, & shakes
Her hollow womb, & clasps the solid stem:
Her bosom swells with wild desire:
And milk & blood & glandous wine.

The Two Songs

I heard an Angel Singing
When the day was springing:
"Mercy, pity, and peace,
Are the world's release."
So he sang all day
Over the new-mown hay,
Till the sun went down,
And the haycocks looked brown.
I heard a devil curse
Over the heath and the furse:
"Mercy vould be no more
If there were nobody poor,
And pity no more could be
If all were happy as ye:
And mutual fear brings peace,
Misery's increase
Are mercy, pity, and peace."
At his curse the sun went down,
And the heavens gave a frown.

The Tyger

Tyger! Tyger! burning bright,
In the forests of the night,
What immortal hand or eye
Could frame thy fearful symmetry?
In what distant deeps or skies
Burnt the fire of thine eyes?
On what wings dare he aspire?
What the hand dare sieze the fire?
And what shoulder, & what art,
Could twist the sinews of thy heart?
And when thy heart began to beat,
What dread hand? & what dread feet?
What the hammer? what the chain?
In what furnace was thy brain?
What the anvil? what dread grasp
Dare its deadly terrors clasp?
When the stars threw down their spears,
And water'd heaven with their tears,
Did he smile his work to see?
Did he who made the Lamb make thee?
Tyger! Tyger! burning bright
In the forests of the night,
What immortal hand or eye
Dare frame thy fearful symmetry?

The Voice Of The Ancient Bard

Youth of delight, come hither,
And see the opening morn,
Image of truth new born.
Doubt is fled, & clouds of reason,
Dark disputes & artful teazing.
Folly is an endless maze,
Tangled roots perplex her ways.
How many have fallen there!
They stumble all night over bones of the dead,
And feel they know not what but care,
And wish to lead others, when they should be led.

The Wild Flower's Song

As I wandered the forest,
The green leaves among,
I heard a Wild Flower
Singing a song.
'I slept in the earth
In the silent night,
I murmured my fears
And I felt delight.
'In the morning I went
As rosy as morn,
To seek for new joy;
But oh! met with scorn.'

Three Things To Remember

A Robin Redbreast in a cage,
Puts all Heaven in a rage.
A skylark wounded on the wing
Doth make a cherub cease to sing.
He who shall hurt the little wren
Shall never be beloved by men.

To Autumn

O Autumn, laden with fruit, and stainèd
With the blood of the grape, pass not, but sit
Beneath my shady roof; there thou may'st rest,
And tune thy jolly voice to my fresh pipe,
And all the daughters of the year shall dance!
Sing now the lusty song of fruits and flowers.
    'The narrow bud opens her beauties to
The sun, and love runs in her thrilling veins;
Blossoms hang round the brows of Morning, and
Flourish down the bright cheek of modest Eve,
Till clust'ring Summer breaks forth into singing,
And feather'd clouds strew flowers round her head.
    'The spirits of the air live on the smells
Of fruit; and Joy, with pinions light, roves round
The gardens, or sits singing in the trees.'
    Thus sang the jolly Autumn as he sat;
Then rose, girded himself, and o'er the bleak
Hills fled from our sight; but left his golden load.

To Morning

O holy virgin! clad in purest white,
Unlock heav'n's golden gates, and issue forth;
Awake the dawn that sleeps in heaven; let light
Rise from the chambers of the east, and bring
The honey'd dew that cometh on waking day.
O radiant morning, salute the sun
Rous'd like a huntsman to the chase, and with
Thy buskin'd feet appear upon our hills.

To Nobodaddy

Why art thou silent & invisible
Father of jealousy
Why dost thou hide thyself in clouds
From every searching Eye
Why darkness & obscurity
In all thy words & laws
That none dare eat the fruit but from
The wily serpents jaws
Or is it because Secresy
gains females loud applause

To See

To see a world in a grain of sand,
And a heaven in a wild flower,
Hold infinity in the palm of your hand
And eternity in an hour.

To Spring

O thou with dewy locks, who lookest down
Thro' the clear windows of the morning, turn
Thine angel eyes upon our western isle,
Which in full choir hails thy approach, O Spring!
The hills tell each other, and the listening
Valleys hear; all our longing eyes are turned
Up to thy bright pavilions: issue forth,
And let thy holy feet visit our clime.
Come o'er the eastern hills, and let our winds
Kiss thy perfumed garments; let us taste
Thy morn and evening breath; scatter thy pearls
Upon our love-sick land that mourns for thee.
O deck her forth with thy fair fingers; pour
Thy soft kisses on her bosom; and put
Thy golden crown upon her languished head,
Whose modest tresses were bound up for thee.

To Summer

O thou who passest thro' our valleys in
Thy strength, curb thy fierce steeds, allay the heat
That flames from their large nostrils! thou, O Summer,
Oft pitched'st here thy goldent tent, and oft
Beneath our oaks hast slept, while we beheld
With joy thy ruddy limbs and flourishing hair.
Beneath our thickest shades we oft have heard
Thy voice, when noon upon his fervid car
Rode o'er the deep of heaven; beside our springs
Sit down, and in our mossy valleys, on
Some bank beside a river clear, throw thy
Silk draperies off, and rush into the stream:
Our valleys love the Summer in his pride.
Our bards are fam'd who strike the silver wire:
Our youth are bolder than the southern swains:
Our maidens fairer in the sprightly dance:
We lack not songs, nor instruments of joy,
Nor echoes sweet, nor waters clear as heaven,
Nor laurel wreaths against the sultry heat.

www.ingramcontent.com/pod-product-compliance
Lightning Source LLC
LaVergne TN
LVHW050407160726